PICTORIAL HISTORY of CUMNOCK

Dane Love

COVER:
Oil Painting of Old Cumnock
by Hugh Rankin

PICTORIAL HISTORY SERIES

uniform with this book

PICTORIAL HISTORY OF DUNDONALD
R. KIRK - ISBN 0-907526-39-X

PICTORIAL HISTORY OF GALSTON
J. MAIR — ISBN 0-907526-37-3

PICTORIAL HISTORY OF NEWMILNS
J. MAIR — ISBN 0-907526-34-9

PICTORIAL HISTORY OF DARVEL
J. MAIR — ISBN 0-907526-40-3

PICTORIAL HISTORY OF DUMFRIES
J. MACKAY — ISBN 0-907526-45-4

PICTORIAL HISTORY OF KILMARNOCK
J. MALKIN — ISBN 0-907526-42-X

PICTORIAL HISTORY of CUMNOCK

Dane Love

Alloway Publishing

First Published in 1992
by Alloway Publishing Ltd.,
Darvel, Ayrshire.

Printed in Scotland
by Walker & Connell Ltd.,
Hastings Square,
Darvel, Ayrshire.

ISBN No. 0-907526-54-3

INTRODUCTION

The change in the face of Cumnock is one which has always fascinated me, particularly since I am still quite young and do not myself remember many of the old landmarks. A few, such as MacCubbin's corner, Mario Luni's, the Bute Hospital and the Parish School, I do recall, but they are just childhood memories, places I passed en route to school. Folk older than I am will no doubt have similar early memories, of shops which have long-since changed hands, buildings which have been demolished, or of people long since passed away. This book will no doubt be a catalyst to the memory banks of the mind, stirring conversations about the "good old days" (which seem to refer to the youth of the folk who recall them) and creating arguments about who lived there or worked here. It is intended as a serious history as well, for though many folk recognise the old street layouts, few are particularly knowledgable about dates and facts, names and prices. Hopefully this volume will help the present residents of the town to appreciate the early history of the place, preserving those buildings with which the original residents would be familiar.

Much has changed in Cumnock over the last thirty years or so. The 1960s was a period of sudden growth, when the council laid plans for a far greater community. However, a number of the old corners of the burgh were lost forever, and the town grew to cover what had been rural fields. There will be many folk who enjoy this fond look back at the old town.

Those wanting to find out more about the history of Old Cumnock parish will wish to refer to the following books: *The History of Old Cumnock* by John Warrick, 1899; *The Cumnocks, Old and New* by Helen Steven, 1899; *Illustrated Guide to Cumnock* by J.P. Ballantine, 1915; *The New History of Cumnock* by John Strawhorn, 1966; or *Cumnock and New Cumnock in Old Picture Postcards* by John Laurenson, 1983. These books and many others, as well as various unpublished sources, have been referred to by myself in the compilation of this book.

I wish to acknowledge assistance I have had in putting this book together from the following people: Sheena Andrew, Myra Cleland, Grace Coburn, Cumnock and Doon Valley District Library Service, William Girvan, Kyle and Carrick District Library Service, John Laurenson, Jean Laurie, Alex Lennox, John Merry, James Quinn, George Scott, Jean Smith, Edith Stevenson and the late John Stirling.

Dane Love   Cumnock, 1992.

*The arms of the Burgh of Cumnock and Holmhead as recorded by
the Court of the Lord Lyon.
Lyon Register, Volume XLI, page 127, 18th August 1959.*

HISTORICAL SKETCH

The name Cumnock is one of considerable antiquity. In fact, it is so old that its original meaning has long-since been forgotten, and historians find great difficulty in agreeing which version has most weight. Revd. John Warrick, whose *History of Old Cumnock*, published in 1899, was for long the standard work on the parish, lists three different interpretations of the name - *Com-cnoc*, a tautological hybrid of Cymric and Gaelic meaning hollow of the hill, certainly an accurate description. However, as this would be pronounced Cumnóck it is an unlikely explanation. His second derivation, *Cumar-oich*, is old Gaélic for meeting of the waters, a widely held belief behind the meaning. The third possibility, *Cam-cnoc*, is Gaelic for bent or crooked hill, and is more preferable according to Warrick. However, over the last ninety years a fourth suggestion has arrived, *Cumanag*, Gaelic for "Little Shrine."

This Little Shrine derivation has possibilities, for in olden days the community hereabouts was known as Cumnock Kirk, as opposed to Cumnock Castle, the name at the time for New Cumnock. New Cumnockians often take delight in telling that New Cumnock is older than Old Cumnock, a statement that is no doubt true as far as the first dwellings are concerned. At New Cumnock a castle was erected in the Middle Ages, probably replacing an earlier Norman motte. This was located on an island in the middle of Loch Cumnock. Known as Cumnock Castle, it seems to have fallen into ruins by 1580, was rebuilt sometime after and was again in ruins by the end of the 18th century. The castle was plundered of stone for other buildings, leaving just a few earthworks still discernible, and the name survives as the village's main street.

There had been residents in the district long before the castle was built. At Boreland in 1892 excavations unearthed Bronze Age burial urns, dated to around 1800 BC. Perhaps from the same period is the possible burial cairn which stood on Coila Hill. Other Bronze Age remains can be found in the immediate vicinity of the parish, such as the Rocking Stone at Lugar, or the burial cairns on the Muirkirk moors.

The Romans passed this way sometime around 100-200 AD although no remains of their road-building or fort-erecting survive in the parish. A claim that there was once a Roman Fort on the summit of Coila Hill (part of Avisyard Hill) is now discounted. Roman roads survive to the north of the area (in the Irvine Valley) and to the south (in Nithsdale), so it is probable that soldiers at least passed through the district. Certainly, a Roman coin was found in the town. Recent aerial surveys have discovered a Roman Road as far up Nithsdale as New Cumnock, with a fort at Corsencon.

The Parish and Barony of Cumnock comprised the present Old and New Cumnock parishes, a total of 62,567 acres, and was owned by the Dunbar family, though they may not have been the original owners. The Dunbars of Cumnock was one of the senior branches of the Dunbars of that Ilk. Indeed, following the extinction of the chiefly line, the chiefship is held by the representative of the Cumnock and Mochrum line, Sir Jean Dunbar, 13th Baronet of Mochrum, resident in America.

Apart from Cumnock Castle, there were six other castles in the barony, of which only Terringzean survives in ruins. Boreland and Leifnoreis castles (located in Old Cumnock Parish) have long since disappeared, the former just a low mound in a field, the latter removed when Dumfries House was erected. In New Cumnock Parish castles also existed at Knockshinnoch, Hall of Auchincross, and Waterhead, fragments of the latter still surviving.

Boreland Castle, originally a timber building on a motte, is thought to have been held by the baron's representative. By 1400 it was occupied by the Hamiltons and then through marriage by the Montgomeries. George Hamilton of Boreland fought with the Earl of Lennox at the Battle of the Butts, near Glasgow, in 1543. A stone with the initials HM and MH and date 1677 was taken from the castle and built into the cottage at Boreland Smithy. The initials are those of Hugh Montgomerie of Prestwickshaws and his wife, Margaret Hamilton, heiress of the estate. At Chapelhouse stood a small chapel associated with the castle. Built into the wall of the ruined cottage is an old graveslab from a child's coffin. The lands of Boreland were purchased by the Earl of Dumfries in 1790.

Leifnoreis, or Lochnorris as it was sometimes spelled, is first noted in 1440 when it was owned by the Craufuirds. They built a new stone tower and remained in ownership until 1635 when it was bought by the Earl of Dumfries. In 1578 George Craufuird was given custody of James Elliot, a noted Border robber, but allowed him to escape. He was to appear before the Privy Council but did not show, so was fined £2000 as an "exemplis of utheris." In 1609 George Craufuird, heir apparent, was imprisoned at Blackness Castle for bearing arms and resetting fugitives. The stones from the castle were used when the present Dumfries House was erected. The site of the castle was excavated in 1897 by Lord Bute, but later covered over.

Terringzean, which has been spelled numerous ways but which is pronounced "Tringan", dates from the early 15th century. More information regarding it will be found in the photographic section. A further fortified site may have existed in the parish. The Mote Hill, located through the Bank Viaduct and which is virtually surrounded by the Lugar Water, may have been an early Norman stronghold.

During the Wars of Independence, when the patriots Wallace and Bruce campaigned against the English, Cumnock played a part, being mentioned a few times, mainly the castle, but also the kirk, in early accounts. Edward I of England passed through the clachan on 1st September 1298, six weeks after his victory at Falkirk. Robert the Bruce came to Cumnock on more than one occasion, according to the poet Barbour, and is supposed to have fooled his captured hound from sniffing his trail by wading an arrowshot's length in one of the local rivers. In 1307 Edward II of England resided in Cumnock Castle, at that time in English hands.

The earliest reference to the kirk at Cumnock is dated 1275. In that year the Rectory of Cumnock was liable to pay £16 tax towards the Bagimond Roll. The kirk stood where the present Old Kirk stands, in the middle of the Square which at the time was the parish burial ground. A few buildings were erected around it, their backs to the kirkyard.

On 27th September 1509 Cumnock was created a Burgh in Barony for James Dunbar of Cumnock, "to be called the Burgh of Cumnock in perpetuity." The charter, issued by King James IV, allowed the establishment of a market, and the inhabitants to "buy and sell in the said burgh wine, wax, pitch and bitumen, woollen and linen cloth, both broad and narrow, wool, skins, oxhides, salt, butter, cheese, and all other kinds of merchandise, together with power and liberty to possess and keep in the said burgh bakers, braziers, tanners, butchers, sellers of flesh and fish, and all other tradesmen belonging to the liberty of a burgh in barony."

The charter allowed the holding of an annual fair on St Matthew's Day, and for eight days thereafter, and for the holding of markets on the Saturday of each week. The charter also makes the first reference to a Market Cross, but the cross of the 16th century no longer survives, if there ever was one, the existing cross being erected in 1703.

The present Market Cross has occupied a number of positions within the burgh. Originally it stood in Townhead Street, the site marked by a cross of cobbles in the roadway. When the Square was converted from a burial ground into a public roadway around 1768 the cross was relocated there, in the north-east corner, adjacent to the Barrhill entry, where it is shown on a map of 1769. It is thought that it was moved

to a position in front of the church door in 1778, the year inscribed on the cross as the date it was repaired. On the finial at the head of the cross are the arms of the Earl of Dumfries, with the Crichton motto, "God Send Grace", and a sundial. For a number of years the ball finial was surmounted by an incandescent gas lamp, removed in 1911. When the Square was partly closed to traffic in 1974 the cross was again restored and moved to its present position, in the south-west corner.

At the beginning of the 16th century there were many notable incidents affecting the burgh. In 1513 the local laird, Sir David Dunbar was killed at the Battle of Flodden along with the Scottish king James IV and many other lairds. In 1512 Patrick Dunbar of Corsencon was murdered in the parish kirk whilst attending mass. For this Andrew Campbell was hanged, though other accomplices, including Robert Campbell, Laird of Schankstoune, escaped. In 1526 the Earl of Cassillis was killed at Prestwick by a group of 1400 men including Craufuird of Leifnoreis.

At the Reformation in 1560 the locality was fiercely protestant, Alexander Dunbar of Cumnock having been denounced a rebel in 1551 for assisting one of Cardinal Beaton's assassins. The parish priest, John Dunbar, was removed from his charge, but was allowed to occupy the manse until his death. Cumnock was served by John Inglis of Ochiltree until 1572 when the first protestant minister, Revd. John Rynd, was appointed.

Around the year 1600 the plague arrived in Cumnock, supposedly brought by two travelling salesmen who were refused entry to Ayr. Many townsfolk died, the kirkyard so full that a mass grave was created at Greenbraehead, the site of the present Central Garage.

The Crichtons of Sanquhar bought the Barony of Cumnock in 1629. In 1622 they had been raised to the peerage with the title Viscount Ayr. In 1633 Lord Ayr was created Earl of Dumfries, one of the subsidiary titles of which is Lord Crichton of Cumnock.

In 1650 the parish of Cumnock was divided into two, creating the parishes of Old and New Cumnock. The latter was by far the larger, but it had the poorest ground. In 1667 the parishes were rejoined, following Lord Dumfries's intervention, but in 1691 the division was again created, remaining thus since. Old Cumnock parish comprises 14,169 acres, New Cumnock 48,165 acres.

The years of struggle for the Covenant affected Cumnock a great deal. The parish seems to have been strongly pro-Covenant. The minister, Revd. John Cunningham, refused to conform to King Charles II's episcopal church and so in 1662 was removed from the church and evicted from his manse. His place was filled by curates, ministers appointed who adhered to episcopacy. In the same year Patrick Crawford of Cumnock was fined £2000 Scots and John Campbell of Glaisnock fined £480 Scots for refusing to conform. It was common to fine the landed gentry whereas the poorer members of society were executed.

In 1666 an uprising broke out in St John's Town of Dalry whereupon followers of the Covenant marched northwards to Mauchline and Ochiltree, reaching Cumnock on 23rd November. Some locals joined the parade, by now 900 strong, and went with them towards Edinburgh where they were beaten back at the Battle of Rullion Green (in the Pentland Hills) by General Hamilton of Dalziel. A few prisoners were taken, among them George Crawford, weaver in Cumnock, executed in Edinburgh on 14th December 1666, and Patrick MacNaught, indicted in 1667, for being "with the rebels at Mauchline in arms and at Pentland."

In 1678 soldiers from Caithness were brought to the parish to seek out the rebels. Known as the "Highland Host", they were most unwelcome, being lodged with the residents. An account of the unpaid lodging and damages inflicted by these men for the year was as follows:

The Parishes of Cumnock, Old and New, sustained of loss by quartering two hundred and fifty Caithness men, fifteen nights, with some officers, £1093 6 8
Extracted by their officers and cleared off their quarters as appears from their notes, 200 0 0
Item, dry quarters to some officers, 64 0 0
Free quarters to them, 60 0 0
Plunder by these soldiers, 958 17 4
By quartering ninety-five of Caithness men six nights, 171 0 0
By quartering three hundred and twenty Caithness men one night, 96 0 0
Dry quarter and plunder by these, 372 2 4
Extendeth to £3015 6 4.

A number of locals took part in the Battle of Bothwell Bridge on 22nd June 1679. John Gemmill and James Mirrie were taken prisoner and sentenced to banishment in America. *The Crown* sailed from Leith with hundreds of prisoners but was shipwrecked in the Orkney islands. The hatches being battened down, most Covenanters drowned, the two Cumnockians amongst them.

On 5th May 1684 a list of "persons who were supposed to have been under arms, or to have harboured those who were," was drawn up and issued by Charles II. Under the parish of Cumnock (at that time comprising Old and New) were listed:

Mr John Halbert in Cumnock forfeited.
James Mitchell, cordiner there.
——————— Crichton in Craigman.
Patrick Gemmil in the old Castle of Cumnock.
William Stillie there.
John Reid in———————
Alexander Stillie in Townhead of Cumnock.
John Tennant at the old castle of Cumnock.
James Dalziel near the kirk of Cumnock.
John Wood, son to Hugh Wood in Lowis.
William Lambie in Polquhays.
James Steel, tenant to Carleton.
George Gemmil in Minaucht.

——————— Greig there.
Robert Murdoch in Knockmarnoch.
John MacKechan in Auchingibbat.
James Wilson at the old castle of Cumnock.
William Skilling in Pablow.
John Campbell in Townhead of Cumnock.
Elsewhere in the document we find reference to:
Robert M'Gavin in Cumnock.
William Campbell in Townhead of Cumnock.
John Weir, tailor in Cumnock.

The Killing Times of 1685 which followed saw a number of locals murdered for their Covenanting adherences. Robert Mitchell, who belonged to the town, was shot at Ingliston Mains, near Moniaive. Thomas Richard, aged 80, was brought from his farm of Greenock Mains, near Muirkirk, to Cumnock and executed in the Square. The bullet ricocheted and pitted a building at the foot of the Barrhill Road, the mark long pointed out thereafter. David Dun and Simon Paterson were captured on Corsegellioch Hill and executed in the town, being buried alongside Richard at the gallows knowe as a mark of disrespect.

In 1686, when Revd. Alexander Peden died at Tenshillingside on Auchinleck estate, he was buried in Auchinleck kirkyard. However, after forty days his body was exhumed by the soldiers and brought to Cumnock where they planned to hang the corpse on the gibbet. Lady Dumfries intervened, but the body was still buried at the gallows tree "out of contempt."

On 19th June 1688 the Revd. David Houston was being transported from Ayr to Edinburgh by a party of dragoons who stopped at the Blue Tower in Cumnock's Tower Street to spend the night. Word reached the local adherents who staged an ambush at the Bello Path on the following day. Houston was injured in the affray but escaped. John MacGeachan of Meikle Auchingibbert, named in the above list, was injured but managed to crawl home. He was hidden in a turf shelter at Stonepark where he died three weeks later and was buried on the spot.

Within a few months the Glorious Revolution brought an end to the years of struggle. The Revd. Francis Fordyce, the government appointed curate, was forced out of the parish kirk and in the kirkyard ninety men tore his gown and told him not to return.

Some of the more extreme Covenanters did not return to the parish kirk and created a Praying Society which met at Wallaceton farm, near Lugar. In 1733 they adhered to the Secession Church and in 1756 built for themselves a kirk and manse at The Rigg. However, the Secession kirk was divided between Anti-Burghers and Burghers, the Rigg kirk being Anti-Burgher in adherence. The Burghers met in Cumnock, originally in the open air, but in 1775 they bought ground in the Tanyard on which they hoped to build a church. Lord Dumfries refused to sell them sand, but at night the Glaisnock flooded and a plentiful supply of it was left in the foundations when the waters receded. This was esteemed as the Cumnock

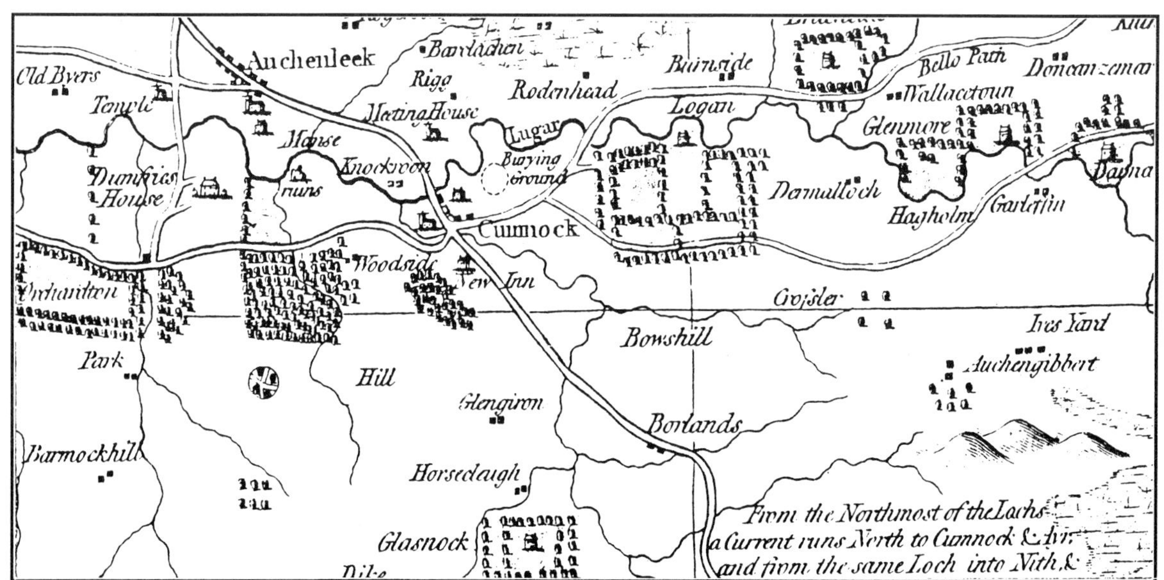

Communion Token from the parish church, 1756.

miracle. The first minister, Revd. James Hall, was only 20 years old when he was appointed, and is thought to have had Robert Burns stay with him on at least one occasion.

The 18th century, following the Union of Parliaments in 1707, was one of great progress in the parish. Penelope succeeded as Countess of Dumfries in her own right, and her marriage to the second son of the Earl of Stair increased the family fortunes. Her eldest son, William, succeeded in 1742 and began making improvements to his estates. Around Leifnoreis and Terringzean castles he planted many new woods and laid out pleasure grounds, creating the landscape with which we are now familiar. The Dettingen Wood he named to commemorate the battle in which he played a part in 1743. A similar round wood was named Stairhill, with Dettingen indicating the positions adopted by the opposing armies. Leifnoreis Castle was demolished, and a magnificent classical mansion erected near the same site, named Dumfries House from his title. It was he who established the limeworks at Benston, used for improving grasslands, and in 1767 sank a coal mine at Garlaff. He died childless in 1768.

One of Lord Dumfries's improvements concerned the whole village. He had the old kirkyard in the Square closed in 1768, replacing it with a new cemetery at the Gallows Knowe, where Peden and others were buried. In the Square

he built a new church, by the same architects as his mansion, John and Robert Adam, and removed the tombstones in order to create public roadways round the kirk. Previously the main road from north to south had crossed the Stepends Ford (bridged in 1753), passed up Lugar Street, turned into Bank Lane, left at the Pawn Steps, then along Tower Street and Townhead Street, past Barshare and Craigens and thence to New Cumnock. For Ayr a branch left the Pawn Steps and went to the Dub Ford, for Muirkirk a roadway left Townhead Street east of the town and passed Drumbrochan. Around 1770 a new roadway was created in a more direct line for New Cumnock, the present Glaisnock Street, and a new way to Muirkirk via the Barr Hill.

The 6th Earl was active in the House of Lords and continued making improvements to the estate. He brought James Taylor from Leadhills to the town in 1790 to be the manager of his mining ventures. Taylor is noted as the original inventor of steam navigation, assisting William Symington to make a paddle-driven boat which sailed on Dalswinton Loch in 1788, Robert Burns being a passenger. Taylor surveyed the Dumfries estate, and suggested where mines could be sunk, quarries opened up, and even proposed an ironworks at Pennyfadzeoch, with water-power via an aqueduct cut from the Loch o' the Lowes. Many of these schemes failed to come to fruition, but Taylor set up the Cumnock Pottery in 1791. Originally intended to make crucibles for foundries, the supply of suitable clay was limited, so more ordinary earthenware pots were made. The pottery failed to make a profit until 1812. Taylor died on 18th September 1825 and is buried in the old cemetery. The Government granted his widow a pension for his services to the country.

The pottery was taken over by the Nicol family. Old Mr Nicol was followed by his son, William, and stepson, David

Cumnock and District on Armstrong's 1775 Map of Ayrshire.

Dunsmuir. Cumnock Pottery developed the "Scotch Motto Ware" which sold extensively in the 19th century. This was pottery items on which mottoes were written, often relevant to the piece, such as "Tak yer wull o' the jam" on a jam pot, "Help yersel' an' dinna be blate" on a sugar bowl, or "Tak anither egg" on an egg-cup. The pottery ceased manufacture in 1907, but continued to sell china and other earthenware from different sources for at least twenty years thereafter.

Robert Burns is not generally thought to have had many Cumnock associations. The Revd. James Hall has been mentioned, and "Winsome Willie" will be detailed in the photographic section. Another friend of the poet was John Kennedy, factor on Dumfries estate from 1783-1793. He was a relation of Mrs Hamilton's, wife of Burns' landlord at Mauchline, and later worked as factor to Lord Breadalbane. Burns wrote to him on many occasions, enclosing copies of his poems, one of which is entitled "To John Kennedy." Kennedy was a subscriber to the Kilmarnock edition. He died in 1812 and was buried in New Calton cemetery, Edinburgh.

Patrick Douglas of Garrallan was another associate. It was he who arranged for Burns to emigrate to Jamaica where he was to work as book-keeper on his estate. However, with the success of the Kilmarnock poems Burns decided to remain in Scotland. Annie Rankine, born near Tarbolton, was the subject of "Corn Rigs". She married John Merry, innkeeper in Cumnock, and was buried in the Barrhill cemetery in 1843.

On 5th May 1800 eighty-two residents in the town signed a document drawn up by Revd. Dr Miller of the parish church. This regulated the number of drinks one was allowed at funerals, for previously these occasions proved to be riotous. The bond survives, now in the Baird Institute, the first rule of it as follows:

COVENANT OF HOUSEHOLDERS REGARDING THE METHOD OF CONDUCTING FUNERALS.

We, Subscribers, being in or near to the village of Cumnock, taking into our serious consideration that, by the present method of conducting burials among us, much time is misspent and money thrown away, and that by entertainments given at many of them the Living are injured and the Dead in many cases dishonoured; and being convinced that a reform is necessary, have agreed and do by our respective subscriptions here annexed agree, bind and oblige ourselves to the Rules or Articles following, viz:-

1 That none of us shall give any general or public entertainment either immediately before or after the Burial of our friends, and that, exclusive of the members of our family and those connected with the chief mourner by blood or relationship, we will not invite any number exceeding 12 to partake of the refreshment that may be provided suitable to the occasion, which we hereby agree shall not exceed 3 glasses of wine, or where this cannot be purchased, one glass of spirituous liquors, and bread proportioned; Binding and obliging ourselves to pay a penalty of Five Shillings sterling in all cases where any of us shall be found to do otherwise.

In 1820 a great epidemic of cholera swept throughout the country and Cumnock did not fail to avoid the devastating effects. Hundreds of people died of the pestilence, the cemetery overflowing with corpses. Around the same time, body-snatching was rife, resulting in the heritors of the parish erecting a wooden hut in the cemetery in order that a constant watch may be made. This was removed in 1869.

The town of Cumnock grew in size in the early 19th century, the population increasing from 787 in 1792 to about 1600 in 1831. Most incomers set themselves up in business as weavers, there being over 120 looms working in the 1830's. Most weaving was done in the Townhead, where a long street of typical weaver's cottages was erected - single storey thatched buildings with one room set aside to hold the loom. Other centres of weaving were New Bridge Street and the separate Bridgend cottages (near Bankend) which had 9 looms. In 1793 there were 28 weavers plus a number of apprentices, working a total of 74 looms. The introduction of steam-driven looms, around 1845, resulted in the trade declining, so much so that in 1861 the heritors of the parish agreed to give £50 to provide webs for the unemployed weavers. The Countess of Dumfries erected a "Jenny House" in Lugar Street, in which a jenny for the weaving of silk was located. However, this trade did not survive too long. By the time of Warrick's history (1899) only three weavers still worked at their looms, one in the Townhead, another in Ayr Road, and a third at Roadside.

Also establishing itself was the manufacture of snuff-boxes, which commenced around 1800 and by 1835 employed over a hundred. Cumnock snuff-boxes were noted for their "invisible wooden hinge," invented by a native of the town, William Crawford. In 1825, when the trade was at its peak, a boxmaker could earn £1 1s a week, a significant wage at that time. The parish produced £6000 worth of boxes in 1825, but this fell to £1600 in 1837 and by 1850 the trade was extinct. Other boxmakers in the town included George Buchanan, George Crawford, Adam Crichton, Peter Crichton, James Drummond and Alexander Lammie.

William MacCartney established his engineering works at Burnside (or Greenholm) in the mid 19th century. Others set up works on the Barrhill (Drummond) and at Waterside Place, where Montgomery and Howat built the noted Cumnock Threshing Machine. Andrew the chemist had a lemonade factory in the Tanyard, Messrs Hunter a bicycle factory. Other places of employment included Brown's Laundry, King's Mill, Brown's Mill, the Creamery, and a coachworks at Skerrington Mill.

It was the creation of the ironworks at Lugar and the coming of the railway in 1850 which changed Cumnock from a small rural village into a growing mining community. William Baird and Company had purchased the Muirkirk and Lugar ironworks in 1856. The Lugar works were resited at the top of the Peesweep Brae in 1866 and five furnaces used to smelt iron-ore. This ore was mined locally, mainly on the moors around Darnconner and Cronberry, and using locally mined coal converted into pig iron.

In the immediate vicinity of Cumnock the oldest pits were sunk at Stepends around 1848 (where the shows meet in the Woodroad) and on the Barrhill around 1852 where two pits existed. The Stepends pit mined coal, one of the Barrhill pits mined ironstone, the other both. Later pits were sunk at Templand (creating Strawberry Bing), Townhead (about 1860) and Shankston, the bings of the latter two in recent years removed.

Outwith the town pits were sunk at Garlaff, Dykes (1865), Glengyron (1865), Garrallan (1876), Knockterra (1880), Hindsward (1880), and Whitehill (1897). The miners employed at these pits were housed in miners' rows which were erected near to the pit-heads. Rows were built at

his charge with many of his congregation to form the Free Church. They acquired ground in Ayr Road and within a short time had built themselves a new church and manse. A Free Church School was established, and for many years this was the best educational establishment in the parish. In 1838 a group of men founded the Congregational Church, at first meeting in the Black Bull hall, latterly buying the former parish school in the Square. In 1883 they moved to their new church at Stepends. A group of Roman Catholics arrived in the town and invited priests from Ayr and Kilmarnock to give them services. In 1850 the first Cumnock priest was appointed, holding services in a hall at the Dumfries Arms stables. They later moved into the Black Bull Hall (once the Congregationalists had moved on) and thence to a small chapel above the priest's house on the Barrhill.

By an Act of Parliament of 1845 Parochial Boards were

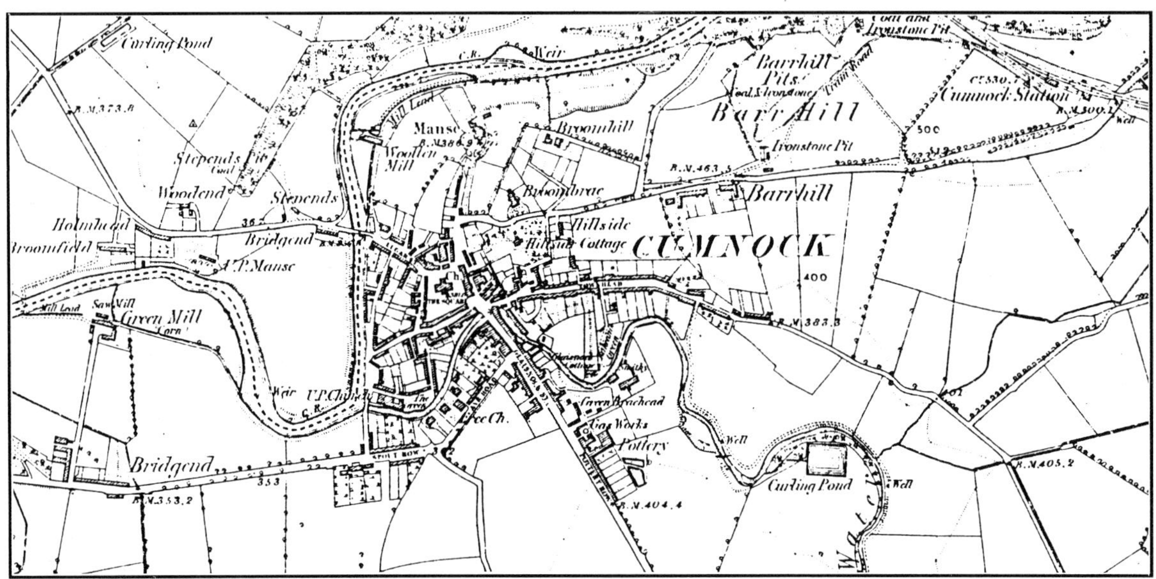

Cumnock as shown on the Ordnance Survey 6" Map of 1860.

Garrallan, Glengyron and Skares, the latter forming the largest community, complete with public hall and reading room, school, and mission hall (1911). 118 houses existed in the rows here, with a few others erected nearby. At Glengyron 44 houses were built behind the railway, let at £4 16s a year. Garrallan had 22 houses, let by the Carriden Coal Company to its employees at 2s 6d per week for a double apartment, 1s 11d for a single.

The works at Lugar continued in use until 1928 but by then the iron-ore was imported from Spain. Coal-mining became the main industry, though over the years it too has declined, so that today there are no mines in the parish, though coal is currently worked by opencast means at Horsecleugh.

The middle part of the 19th century saw a number of splits in the Church of Scotland. In Cumnock, at the Disruption of 1843, the parish minister, Revd. Ninian Bannatyne, left

constituted to run certain local affairs. It maintained the kirk, kirkyard, schools and poor of the parish. The first Inspector of the Poor was James Boyd. A school had been erected in the Square in 1804, complete with schoolroom, gaol and library, but by 1845 it was found to be too small so a new building was erected on the Barrhill, designed by John Baird, and built at a cost of no more than £450. It was opened in May 1847 with David Scott as schoolmaster.

The population of the town continued to rise, reaching around 2600 inhabitants by 1860. Acts of Parliament of 1850 and 1862 allowed "populous places" to set themselves up as Police Burghs. Some townsmen sent a petition to the Sheriff of Ayr in 1866 wishing Cumnock to be created a Police Burgh. It was signed by nine men - David Crichton, William Dalgleish, Daniel King, William Ettershank, David Scott, Duncan Ballantine, John MacCowan, Anthony MacClymont and Alexander Muir. A meeting was held at the Dumfries

Arms on 2nd November 1866, with arguments for and against between the pro- and anti-burgh residents. A vote was held by the inhabitants who had a £10 rental on 5th November and the result was so close that the burgh was agreed to by a majority of three. The for and against factions had many arguments and things were so bad that folk left the church or were put out their homes because they disagreed with the minister or owners. At the fiftieth jubilee of the formation, Provost James Richmond recalled the time, "The day of the election was one of the most turbulent in the history of the town. Those in favour of the Burgh were groaned and hissed at as they passed through the streets, and if any of their family ever went near the window, they were forced to go back by those in the street making faces at them and annoying them in every way possible."

Among those who voted for the burgh were John Templeton, shoemaker, Daniel King, dyer, William Ettershank, banker, John Allan, grain merchant, James Paterson, draper, David Earle, William MacLatchie, wright, Alex Muir, grocer, Thomas Barrowman, miner, John Rankin, painter, George Samson, grocer, Duncan Ballantine, printer, Dr Lawrence, Revd. William Hutton, John Ballantine, photographer, James Murray, innkeeper, Anthony MacClymont, writer, Hamilton Rose, writer, James Dalgleish, millwright, David Scott, teacher, Andrew Murdoch, mason, Andrew White, banker, David Crichton, baker, Hew Crichton, Writer to the Signet, William Dalgleish, draper, John Drummond, millwright, William White, farmer, George Alexander, carrier, Robert Dalgleish, dealer, John MacCowan, innkeeper, David MacLeod, wright, and William MacGavin, miller.

A public election was called and nine men were elected as the first council:

William Dalgleish, draper	20 votes
David Lawson Scott, teacher	20 votes
William MacLatchie, wright	20 votes
Thomas Barrowman, miner	20 votes
Daniel King, wool manufacturer	20 votes
William MacGavin, miller	18 votes
John Drummond, engineer	18 votes
John MacCowan, innkeeper	18 votes
Duncan Ballantine, bookseller	16 votes.

They met at first in the parish school at midday on 10th December but several members could not attend so a second meeting was held three days later, in the evening, when William Dalgleish was appointed Senior Police Magistrate, Daniel King and William MacGavin Junior Magistrates. David Scott was appointed Inspector of Poor on a salary of £4 and Andrew White became the Clerk and Collector on a salary of £15.

The new burgh council began to make improvements to the town and soon it was agreed that it had been the right decision to form a burgh. Gas-lamps were erected to light the streets at night and work commenced on creating a new water supply from Borland reservoir, opened in 1869. Streets were improved and by 1915 tarmacadam was introduced in the busiest parts of the town. Street-cleaning was commenced, the council buying a large two-wheeled barrow to do this. Local bye-laws were created, and to deal with offenders a burgh court was established in 1869. In the same year a burgh slaughterhouse was erected on the Barrhill. In 1870 the council's first case of planning permission occurred, when William MacLatchie's proposals for a building in Waterside Place were passed.

A town hall was erected in 1885 and from then on the council met in chambers there. The first proposals for a burgh hall were made in 1880 but it was not until 8th January 1883 when Lord Bute offered ground and a donation of £500 that fund-raising began in earnest. The foundation stone was laid in October 1883 and the hall opened on 7th June 1885, having cost £3000 to build. It was not until 1896, when a large bazaar was held, that the remaining debt was paid off. The main hall can seat 800, with an additional 100 on a balcony. The Lesser hall, located over what was the Council Rooms and Athenæum Library, can seat 300.

In 1887 the former curling pond at Herdston was altered into a flushing pond which was used to clean out the Glaisnock in dry weather. Four years later the council became responsible for the upkeep of the roads within the burgh.

In 1894 the council created for itself a simple burgh seal which included the market cross with a sheaf of corn to one side, a weaver's shuttle on the other. This insignia was not proper heraldry, but was used until the burgh received a grant of arms from the Lord Lyon in 1959, as shown at the front of this volume. Application was made to the Secretary of State to take over part of Holmhead into Old Cumnock parish, approved on 12th August 1895.

In 1879 James Keir Hardie came to live in Cumnock. He was born illegitimately at Legbranock, near Holytown, in Lanarkshire on 15th August 1856. He worked in the pits there before being sacked for trying to form a trade union. He accepted a call to become the secretary of the Ayrshire Miners' Association, living at first in Waterside Place (now the site of the shopping centre) and later in Barrhill Road. He led the Ayrshire miners in the strike of 1881. In 1882 he became a reporter for the *Cumnock News*, for which he wrote many articles, his own column, and even some poetry:

When the shadows o' the e'enin' mingle wi' the summer gloamin',
And the bairnies tired and wearied frae their play come hirplin'
*   hame;*
Auld grannie, ere she haps them in their cuddle ba' sae cosy,
Kind and couthie draws them near her as she tells them still the
*   same*
Auld story o' the land o' bliss, heaven's happy home abune,
Where the bairnies dwall wi' Jesus freed frae ilka taint o' sin.

Keir Hardie was a devoutly religious man, joining Cumnock Congregational Church on 9th July 1882. However, on 23rd March 1884 he, the minister, Revd. A.N. Scott, and 39 others resigned their membership and set up an Evangelical

Union church in a building in Barrhill Road. Most of these people rejoined the Church after a short time. In 1886 Keir Hardie was appointed organising secretary of the newly founded Ayrshire Miners' Union on a salary of £75 per annum. In 1888 the Scottish Labour Party was formed and in 1892 Keir Hardie was elected M.P. for West Ham. A few months later, in January 1893, the Independent Labour Party was founded with Keir Hardie as national chairman. Hardie lost his seat in 1895 but in 1900 was elected as member for Merthyr in Wales, holding it for the remainder of his life. He died at a nursing home in Glasgow on 26th September 1915, was cremated, but is commemorated on a memorial stone in Cumnock's new cemetery.

In 1895 Old Cumnock Parish Council was created, taking over from the old Parochial Board which was established in 1845 under the Poor Law Act. The council met at first in the Town Hall, but in 1916 moved into their own premises in Ayr Road, now Stevenson's offices. Men who were chairmen of the council were James Gray, David Reid, Robert Livingstone, George MacTurk (twice), George Bridges and John Craig. George MacTurk presided at the last council meeting on 15th May 1930, when Cumnock District Council took over.

The District Council was responsible for a larger area, including Mauchline, Muirkirk and New Cumnock, the first chairman being John Nicol of the Bank School. The council bought Millbank for their offices. George MacTurk was the second chairman, from 1932 until 1935.

In 1872 the Education (Scotland) Act was passed, setting up School Boards in every parish. The new school board in Cumnock was founded in April 1873, the original members being Thomas Barrowman, John Baird, George Samson, George MacKervail, Revd. James Murray, C.G. Shaw and Patrick Boswell of Garrallan, the latter chairman for the first twelve years. At that time the parish school at Broombrae educated 189 pupils, under David Scott, the Free Church School in Ayr Road having 220 pupils under Robert Brown. A private school for girls was also run in Ayr Road, Miss Susan Lamont teaching 27 pupils. Outwith the burgh were schools at Garrallan with 48 pupils and another at Benston with 47 on the roll. Apart from Benston, all the schools were overcrowded, having room for 403 pupils, but with 845 children aged between 5 and 13 in the parish.

The new school board took over the running of the Parish School from the heritors and the Free Church and the two country schools were passed into the board's hands. In the burgh the schools were renamed Cumnock Public School and Ayr Road Public School. The board made plans for the extension of classroom accomodation, both in the town and at Garrallan. The new Cumnock Public School had its foundation stone laid in 1875, the pupils under Mr Scott arriving at their desks in 1876, followed by Mr Brown's pupils in May 1877. The two men became joint headmasters until Scott retired. The new school at Garrallan was likewise opened in 1876 with J.B. Wilson as headmaster.

In 1886 St John's School was opened in Bank Avenue, at which Roman Catholic children were educated. They had previously attended the public school where they were excused Bible lessons, or else the Roman Catholic school at Benston. In 1907 the Marquis of Bute paid for the erection of a replacement for the original wood and iron building. It remained in use until the new St John's Primary School was erected at Barshare. In 1961 some of the pupils left for the new St Conval's High School built at Holmhead. The school was named after the patron saint of Cumnock, Conval, who brought Christianity to the area in the early seventh century.

The new Public School was soon found to be too small to accommodate all the pupils and so the old Parish School was again put to use. Hillside House came on the market and was bought by the school board, being converted into a Higher Grade School, opened in 1911. In 1919 the schools came under the control of the new Ayrshire Education Authority. They again proved to be overcrowded, and the Mission Hall at the foot of the Barrhill was used for additional classrooms. An extension was added to Hillside House, opened in 1926. Hillside House itself was demolished being replaced by a building similar to the extension. In 1927 the school was renamed Cumnock Academy.

In 1952 Greenmill Primary School was built in Ayr Road, opened in 1954. However the Academy on the Barrhill proved to be cramped, with the main road separating the two buildings. In 1965 work commenced on the building of an extension at Greenmill to create a New Academy, as it was long known. The primary school, and the name Greenmill, was transferred to the Barrhill buildings. The new academy was again extended in 1971 with the erection of the Social and Recreation wing. Greenmill as a primary again became cramped, and a second primary school for the town was built at Drumbrochan, confusingly named Barshare Primary School.

Schools elsewhere in the parish were closed, Skares in 1966, Garrallan becoming a special school until its pupils transferred to Cronberry. Cronberry School was closed in 1992, the pupils being rehoused in a new purpose built school erected at Drumbrochan, named Hillside School. Glaisnock House was in 1952 opened as a Rural Junior Secondary School, taking boarders as well as day pupils, specialising in educating farmer's sons. It was closed in June 1973 and later converted to an outdoor centre.

The Census of 1871 found the population of the burgh to be 2,903, increasing to 3,345 in 1881. The population fell for twenty years thereafter mainly due to the lack of sites for building in the burgh, Lord Bute refusing to sell ground. Instead he wished to grant plots on a 99 year lease after which the buildings built thereon became his property. Warrick ends his history of the town by asking "Is it too much to hope that the noble Lord will yet listen to the prayer of the people of Cumnock, and in the exercise of a gracious power, remove the restrictions which have interfered so long with the growth and prosperity of our town?"

Accomodation was something of a problem, many houses being overcrowded or unfit for use. Councillor James Neil proposed the erection of the first housing scheme in the burgh. The first council houses (twelve in number) were erected at Urbana Terrace in 1914 on ground bought from Baird's Trustees, though the war held up progress for a time. They were let in March 1915 at £13 5s per annum for a ground floor house, £13 for an upper floor. In 1915 Thomas Gilchrist was the first soldier from the town to suffer death in the Great War.

When peace resumed, work commenced on more council houses — 36 being built in Cairn Road, Car Road and Shankston Crescent in 1920 and Hall Terrace, Latta Crescent, Gemmell Avenue and Gray Street being erected in 1925. These streets occupied the former Racecourse. In the Square the burgh made arrangements with the Commercial Bank to widen the gap through to Glaisnock Street. A new bank building, with curved facade, was built on the site in 1927. In 1929 more houses were erected in Urbana Terrace, bringing the burgh total to 189.

It was not just the burgh which built new council houses, Ayrshire County Council were also erecting houses in what became the Landward part of the town, mainly to rehouse residents of the older miners' rows. Skerrington Place was thus erected in 1926, the first houses of a larger scheme to be created at Netherthird, some of which were erected by the Scottish Special Housing Association. The County Council also erected houses adjacent to the burgh at Glenramskill, Glencairn and Glenlamont. The burgh's Herdston Place was built in 1932. Electricity arrived in the town from the power station at Kilmarnock in 1928, the first public lights being erected in the Square.

The council enforced compulsory purchase orders to buy ground at Shankston and Keir Hardie Hill from Lord Bute. Emrys Avenue was named after Emrys Hughes, Keir Hardie's son-in-law, and provost at the time. McCall Avenue was named after the convener of the housing committee, Michie Street after the Provost of Renfrew who was arbiter in the inquiry regarding compulsory purchase, and Wyllie Crescent after a government official also involved. With new houses available a start could be made in clearing slums at Elbow Lane, Tanyard, Tower Street, Waterside Place, Donaldson Brae, Strand, Kilnholm Place, Gibb's Close and Manse Lane.

The rise in population resulted in increased membership of the town's churches. The parish kirk was demolished and a new larger building erected in the Square in 1866. On 9th April 1899 the burgh council approved plans for the erection of a Mission Hall in Barrhill Road. The present large Crichton Memorial Church was erected in 1899, the plans for it presented to the council on 11th May 1896. A third Presbyterian congregation met in the United Presbyterian Church, next to the Meetinghouse Bridge. With the union of the U.P. and Free churches in 1900 the burgh had two United Free churches, remaining thus until the U.F. and Established churches rejoined in 1929. This created three Churches of Scotland in Cumnock, the Old, Crichton and West churches, the latter two merging in 1949 to form the present Crichton West Church.

Not everyone in the United Free church agreed to the union with the Established Church and wished to remain independent. There were sufficient numbers to form a congregation of their own, meeting in the Lesser Town Hall until in 1939 they managed to build a church for themselves in Glaisnock Street. The Congregational Church was founded on 28th October 1838 in a hall in the Black Bull Close, later acquiring the old parish school and gaol in the Square. It moved to a new church at Stepends in 1883, the old church sold to the Clydesdale Bank who built their present premises on the site, designed by John Murdoch of Ayr. A number of Baptists moved into the district, building up a sufficient following to appoint their first minister in 1876 and build a church on the Barrhill in 1887. A number of other groups, such as Brethren, met in various halls in the burgh, including the Dumfries Arms Stables, the Close Brethren building a Gospel Hall in Barrhill Road in 1964, the Open Brethren creating a hall on the first floor of a building in the Square. The Salvation Army met in a wooden hut in Townhead Street from 1925 until their present hall was opened on 25th November 1967.

The Roman Catholics met in a number of different places prior to the erection of St John's Church at the top of Glaisnock Street. The 3rd Marquis of Bute, who had turned from Presbyterianism to Catholicism, paid for much of the cost, including the Revd. John O'Neill's stipend.

On 2nd April 1928 Cumnock Municipal Bank was founded, the first directors being Alex Borland, ironmonger, George Bridges, teacher, James Neil, retired, and Emrys Hughes, journalist, the latter chairman. The other three founder shareholders were Allan MacCall, fruit merchant, John Wilson, retired, and George MacTurk, miner's agent. The shareholders did not receive dividends and the directors were unpaid, the profits being passed to the Town Council. By 1960 deposits in the bank amounted to £98,900, with two hundred current accounts, equal to about one account for every eight households in the burgh.

In 1929 Cumnock became a Small Burgh when the Local Government (Scotland) Act renamed Police Burghs as such. At this time the folk outwith the burgh were served either by the county council or by Cumnock District Council. In 1937 the first extension to the burgh's 268 acres took place, when 73 acres of the Woodroad Park were added. A further 157 acres were added to the south in 1957 and 85 acres in 1963.

After the second war, when 461 evacuees arrived in the town from Clydebank and Clydeside, more council houses were erected at Hearth Place, some of them pre-fabricated dwellings. In the 1950s the Glebe was sold by the kirk to the council and sixty houses built round the old manse which was converted into two dwellings. In 1952 work commenced on the Drumbrochan houses and by 1954 the council was proud to unveil a plaque on a house at 2 Holland Crescent to commemorate the erection of the burgh's 1000th council

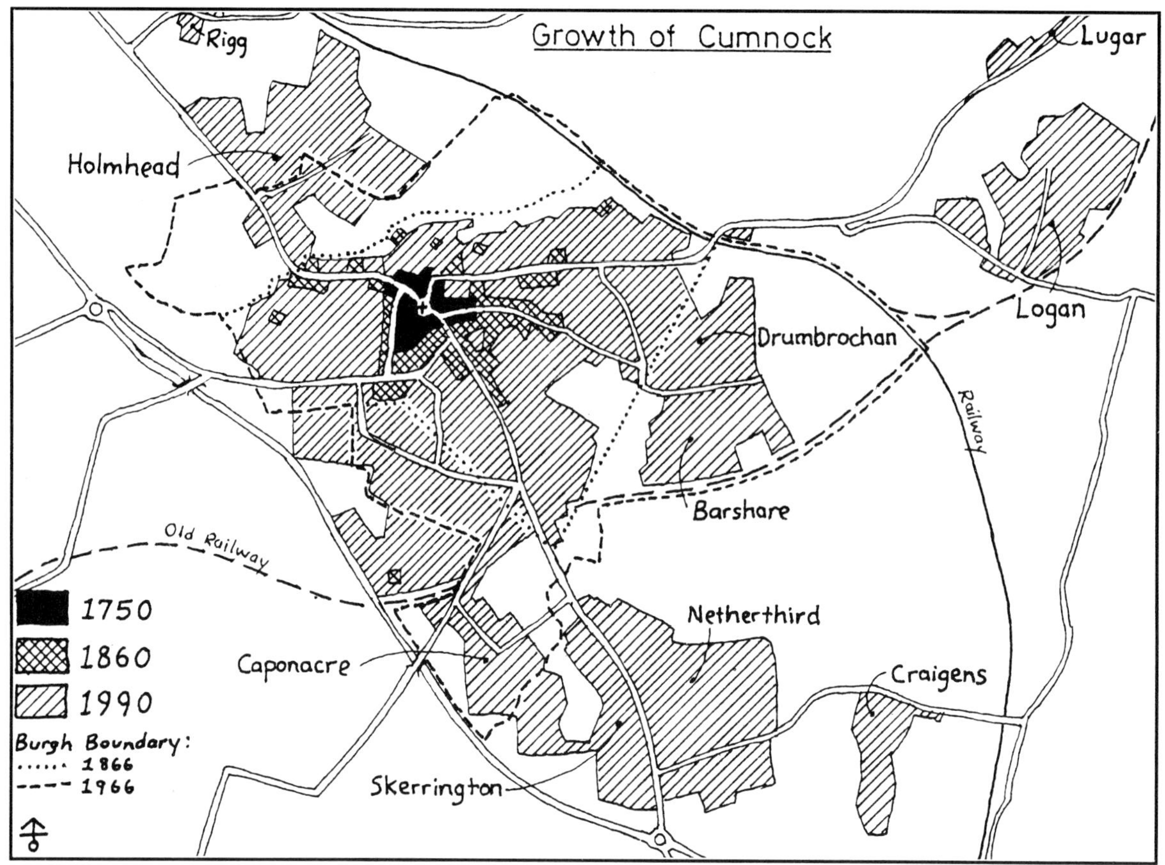

Map of Cumnock showing the growth of the town and the extent of the former burgh.

house. This gave Cumnock the highest percentage of council owned houses in Ayrshire.

Outwith the burgh, but adjoining the town, the county council created new communities in which to house the residents of the mining villages at Skares, Lugar, Cronberry and elsewhere. Logan estate was purchased, the mansion demolished, and a compact village built, the first houses occupied in 1948. The community set up a Tenants Rights Association in 1949 which instituted galas in 1950. The village had a public house (Logangate Arms - 1955), church hall associated with Lugar Parish Church (1959), post office (1962), school (1963), and police station (1967).

A similar community was created at Netherthird, across the road from Skerrington, complete with primary school (1960), St Ninian's Parish Church (1955), community centre (opened 28th June 1957, having cost £10,000) and shops. More remote, and comprised entirely of houses, a community was created at Craigens. In 1959 the burgh signed an overspill agreement with Glasgow to take one thousand families.

In 1959 the Burgh was granted an official coat of arms by the Lord Lyon. This was based on elements of the arms of early owners - the eight roses for Dunbar, the lion rampant halved to indicate Dunbar and Crichton, the cushion for Thomas Randolph, Earl of Moray, the latter placed on a gold field indicative of Dunbar of Cumnock. The motto "Prompt in Progress" echoed the Dunbar motto, "In Promptu." The title "Burgh of Cumnock and Holmhead" was in 1960 shortened to Burgh of Cumnock.

The Prompt in Progress motto was vigourously followed by the council, even to the extent of nonsensical plans. In the late 1940s proposals were made by Ayr County Council and St Andrew's House in Edinburgh for a large new town of 21,000 inhabitants, with houses extending over all the lands of Drumbrochan and Barshare and a new town centre created near Netherthird. The style of architecture was typical of the period, with right-angled blocks of houses, lack of service roads, and few amenities. At the same time the first proposals for a Cumnock by-pass road were mooted, and a proposed road system within the town had Hall Terrace as a major thoroughfare, Townhead Street as a cul-de-sac, and Drumbrochan Road continuing to the Murray Park. The *Chronicle* of 1966 writes, "the powers-that-be safely conjecture that the original 21,000 might be doubled by the 1980's."

Fortunately the council's plans proved to be over ambitious, for the style of building, where erected elsewhere, has generally proved to be unsuccessful, few people wanting to live in such faceless schemes. Instead the new community of Drongan was built and in Cumnock growth was more steady. The new scheme at Barshare was the only part constructed, and the plans were altered as new decades required different styles of housing.

New council houses continued to be erected, the flats and shops in Townhead Street in November 1967. In June

Hunter's Way. Sites of previous buildings were used for development, the former hatchery in Auchinleck Road became Hoyle Crescent, the Bute Hospital Murray Court. Elsewhere Cameron Crescent was built at Skerrington and new bungalows erected in Cairn Road, Holmburn Road and proposed at Bankend.

In 1975 the Local Government (Scotland) Act brought

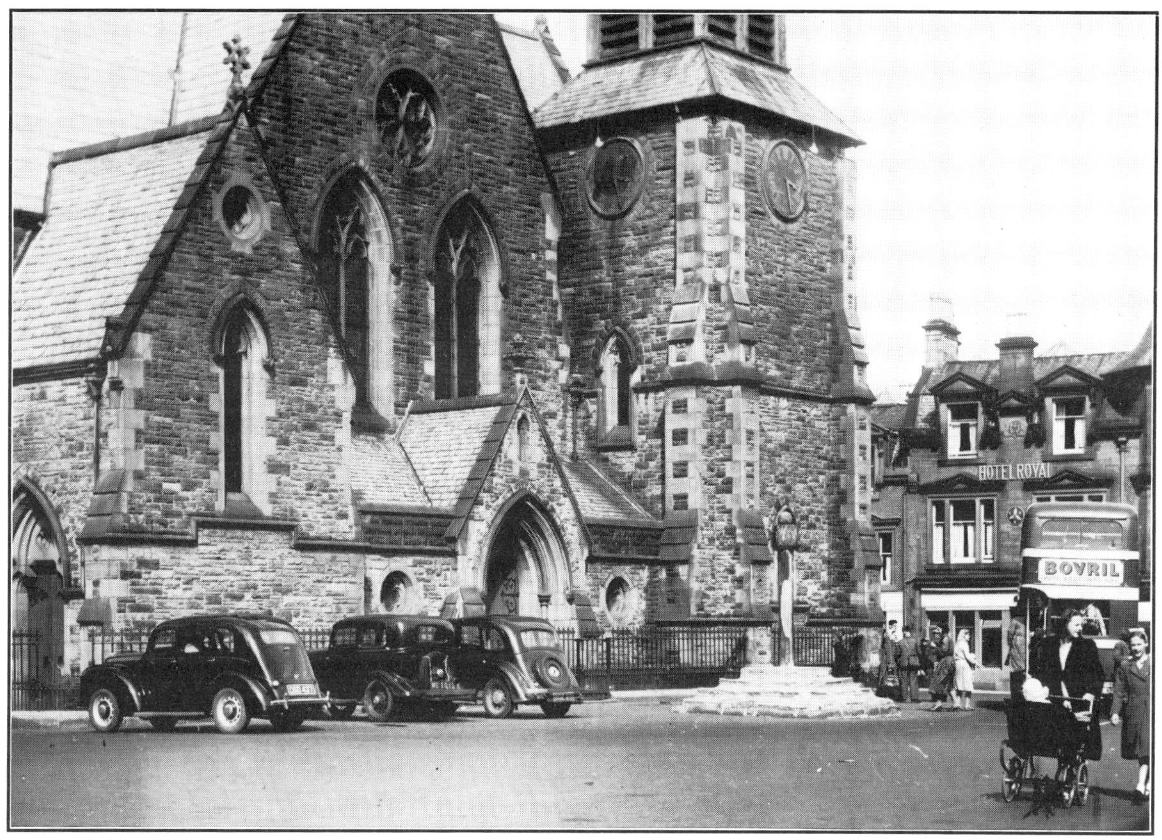

The Square

1970 William Ross, Secretary of State for Scotland, later Lord Ross of Marnock, officially opened the town's 1500th council house, located in a block of 12 flats at Meagher Court. Further flats were built on the site of the New Station in 1970. At Drumbrochan Walker Court, Bannatyne Court and McClymont Court were erected in 1971. Council house building slowed down thereafter, small schemes being built at King's Way, in gap sites on the Barrhill and other small areas.

As council house-building diminished, the erection of private dwellings increased. The first modern group of houses was built in Bank Glen, off Bank Avenue. These were built by David King, who later went on to develop much of the scheme at Holmhead - Holmhead Road, King's Drive, Broomfield Avenue, Oakbank Drive and Banfield Drive. Other private house-builders erected homes at Holmhead, self-build plots sold at Lorimer Crescent, Duncan Court and

regionalisation and the creation of Strathclyde. The old burgh councils were abolished, but Cumnock managed to remain independent of Ayr and became the centre of a new Cumnock and Doon Valley District. Many of the town and former district council's premises in Cumnock were abandoned in favour of a centralised locality at the former Coal Board workshops and offices at Lugar. The Town Hall was no longer used for council meetings and many buildings in the town became surplus to requirements and have yet to find a new purpose.

Much of the town centre has been redeveloped over the years. Many old buildings were cleared away to make the narrow streets and heavily built up nucleus more airy and bright. However, much of the true character of Cumnock was lost at this time, to be replaced with faceless boxes such as the new Police Station (1971) or the Glaisnock Shopping Centre (1975). Some good did come from this developing period, however, the pedestrianisation of part of the Square, the widening of the Tanyard (1966), and the increased facilities for parking, for example, but many felt that the Cumnock they knew and loved was being needlessly thrown away. A number of distinctive buildings were removed, such as the Public School and Bute Hospital on the Barrhill, and there have even been suggestions to demolish the Town Hall! Attitudes are beginning to change, though are doing so slowly, for some older buildings have been cleaned up and rejuvenated.

Industry in the parish has changed over the last thirty years or so. In 1962 a serious collapse of the shaft at Barony Colliery in Auchinleck parish affected many of the residents of Cumnock. The pit had to be closed, and remained thus for a number of years. Not all of the miners could be re-employed in other pits, and many were laid off. The unemployment rate in the district soared, and many families moved elsewhere in the search for work. To help alleviate the problem the government funded the establishment of advance factories, built on the edge of Cumnock in preference to Auchinleck. An industrial estate was formed at Caponacre, and factories erected on other greenfield sites at Skerrington Mains, Ayr Road and Auchinleck Road. At Skerrington the Bata shoe factory was opened in 1964, remaining in that company's hands until 1991. In October 1964 the Sykes chicken hatchery was opened in Auchinleck Road, but it closed in November 1970. In 1967 Gray's carpet factory was built at Caponacre, followed by factories making synthetic fibres in 1967 (Monsanto), clothing (Falmer Jeans), yarns

(Carpet Yarn Spinners) and aircraft parts (Scottish Aviation). Cumnock Knitwear Company set up a factory off Ayr Road in 1960, quickly expanding, as had John Foster's spinning mill in Ayr Road, built in 1948 and extended in 1959. Near Skares a brickwork was established in 1957. The bus garage in Ayr Road was opened in 1954 and new offices for the Ministry of Labour in Ayr Road in 1956.

A number of these factories did not last much more than a decade or so, of the above list only Falmers, Kingsmead carpets (as Gray's became) and Cumnock Knitwear surviving to the present. A number of industries have come and gone in the meantime, such as Stonefield Trucks or Fenner Conveyors. Many of the larger factories were subdivided into smaller units, and even one, the hatchery, was demolished. Small workshops were erected at Caponacre and at Skerrington, diversifying the industries in the town, to create a wider industrial base away from coal-related employment.

The future for Cumnock cannot be predicted. However, it is almost certain that reliance on coal as a means of employment has long gone, certainly to the extent of the past. Newer industries have been introduced, but none employ anything like the same amount of people, meaning that many of the residents of the town must travel to find work, to Ayr, Prestwick, Kilmarnock, Irvine, or even Glasgow. For many people Cumnock has become a dormitory town, though it acts as a market centre for other communities such as New Cumnock, Auchinleck or Muirkirk. The historians of tomorrow will record the outcome.

TERRINGZEAN CASTLE — Pronounced "Tringan", this castle was partly built in the 15th century. The earliest reference to it dates from 1438 when £14 Scots in tax was payable by the "farm lands of Trarynyane in the barony of Cumnok" in order to support the royal household. A charter of 26th April 1467 was awarded to Thomas Boyd, Earl of Arran, of the lands of "Trarinzeane". His wife, Mary, was sister of King James III. The lands were later confiscated when he lost the king's favour and became the property of the Crawfuirds of nearby Leifnoreis. This family renamed the castle Crawfuirdstone for a time. In 1563 they resigned the lordship to Sir Matthew Campbell of Loudoun who signed the Protestant Bond of Union in 1559. Though the lands were bought by Lord Dumfries in 1696, the present Countess of Loudoun has Lady Tarrinzean as a subsidiary title. The castle was excavated in the 1890s by the 3rd Lord Bute and the walls stabilised. The tower, which has walls ten feet thick, is the oldest part. Lesser wings have stood to the north and west of it, creating a courtyard. The castle was partly surrounded by a moat, with steep embankments on the other sides.

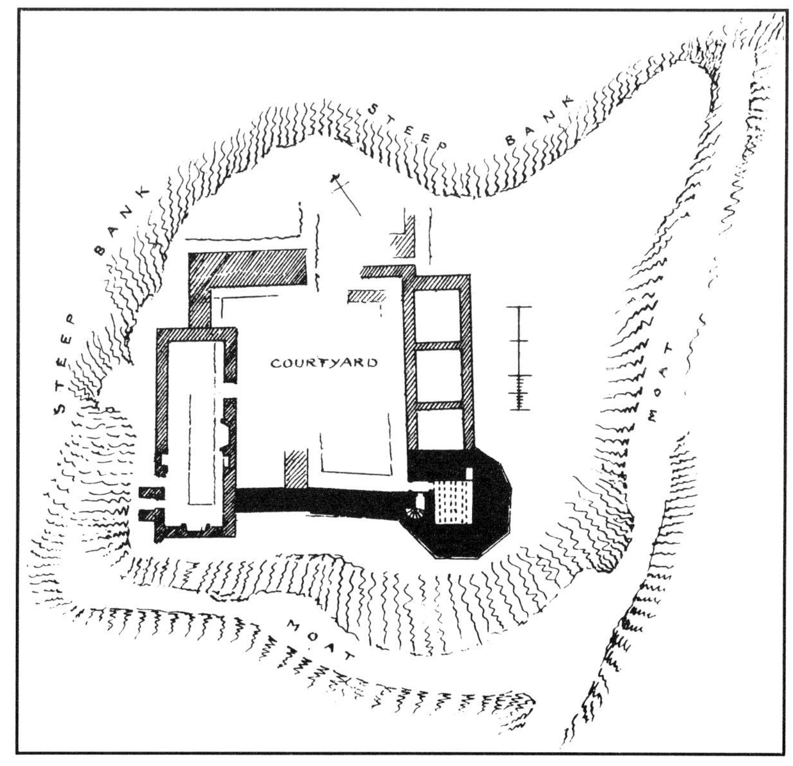

PEDEN'S MONUMENT —The Peden obelisk was erected in 1891 to mark the spot where the "Prophet of the Covenant" was finally buried. It is the third memorial to mark the grave, the two previous stones still surviving. Made from Aberdeen Granite, the memorial was designed by R.S. Ingram and unveiled on 16th July 1892 by Prof John Stuart Blackie. Adjacent to the memorial are the two Peden Thorn trees. Tradition stated that if the branches touched then the soldiers of France would invade Scotland. Trimmed annually, the bushes became old and frail but cuttings were taken from them and replanted.

DUN AND PATERSON'S GRAVE —The inscription on this old tombstone, believed to have been erected by Robert Paterson, the Old Mortality of Sir Walter Scott, reads: HeRe LyeS DAVID DVN AND SIMON PATeRSON WHO WAS SHOT IN THIS PLACE BY A PARTY OF HIGHLANDeRS FOR THEIR ADHeRANCe TO THe WORD OF GOD AND THe COVeNANTeD WORK OF ReFORMATION 1685. Little is known of the two martyrs' history other than the fact that they were shot in the town following their encapturement on Corsgellioch Hill. Dun is said to have come from Closs, in Ochiltree parish, though others say that he came from Selkirkshire.

JOHN MacGEACHAN'S GRAVE — Situated in a small field at Stonepark, this memorial marks the spot where John MacGeachan of Meikle Auchingibbert was buried. The old stone (erected in 1728) is located by the side of the monument erected after a sermon preached here on 28th August 1836. The inscription reads: HERE LIES JOHN M'GEACHAN WHO FOR HIS CONSTANT ADHERENCE TO THE WORD OF GOD PROSECUTING THE ENDS OF OUR NATIONAL LEAGUE AND COVENANT AND APPEARING FOR THE RESCUE OF THE REV DAVID HOUSTON ONE OF THE PERSECUTED MINISTERS OF THE GOSPEL WAS SHOT AT BELLOW PATH BY A PARTY OF BLOODY DRAGOONS XXVIIITH JULY MDCLXXXVIII.

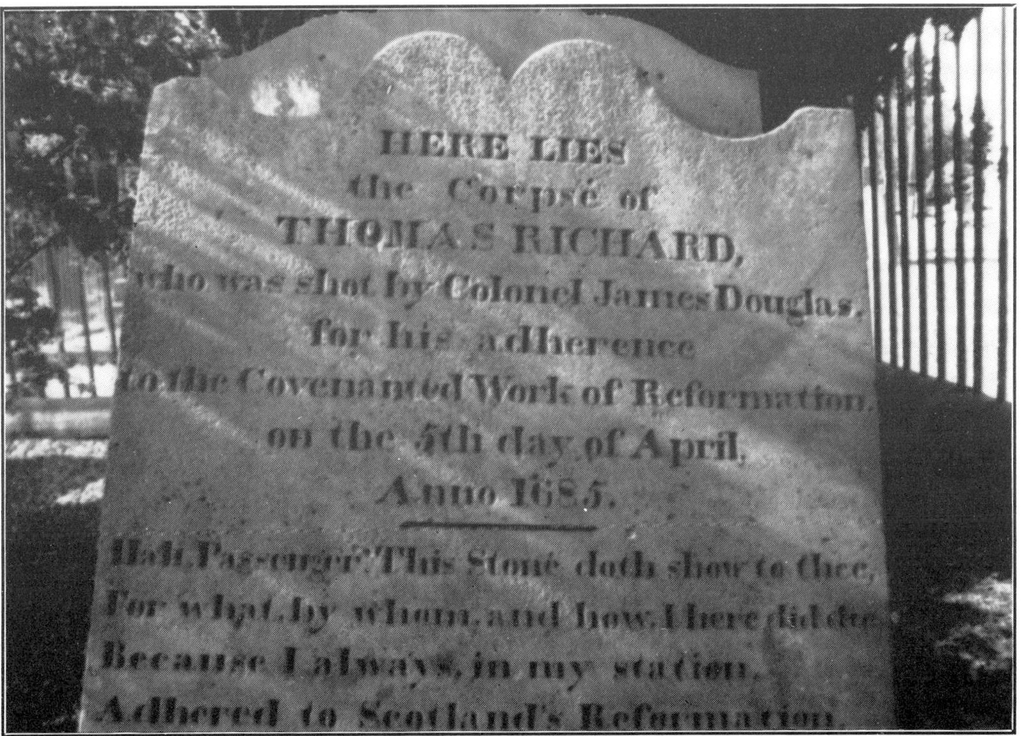

THOMAS RICHARD'S GRAVE — Thomas Richard was the tenant farmer at Greenock Mains, near Muirkirk. At the age of 80 he was taken from his farm by Peter Inglis and brought to Cumnock for trial under Colonel Douglas, brother of the Duke of Queensberry. He was shot in the Square on 5th April 1685, still used as the parish kirkyard. The bullet ricocheted and left a mark on the gable of a building at the foot of the Barrhill until it was demolished. His corpse was taken to the Gallows Knowe for burial, the spot used for interring criminals. He was the first Covenanter to be buried on that spot.

MERCAT CROSS — The market cross was erected in 1703 as a symbol of the Burgh. Whether an earlier cross had existed is unknown. The cross has a plain shaft capped with a cube and ball finial. On the sides of the cube are the arms of the Dumfries family, a sundial, and the legend *1703 REPAIRED 1778*. The cross has stood in various locations over the centuries, from the north-east corner of the Square to Townhead Street, to the front of the kirk door to its present location at the south-western corner of the Square. The cross, a registered Ancient Monument, was restored again in 1974.

MARKET IN THE SQUARE — The Square was used as the main market place of the town from the mid 18th century until the early 20th century. This photograph is dated 1881 when traffic was certainly less of a problem! On the right is the Black Bull Hotel, before the 1906 alterations, and the gable of an earlier thatched Hamilton Place facing the Square. This was the shop of S. Manderson, general outfitter. The shot-hole left at Richard's execution was on this building. The large building to the left was the home of William Hood, ironmaster, before being sold to John Goldie who converted it into a tailors.

DUMFRIES HOUSE — This spectacular mansion was erected between 1754 and 1759 by the 5th Earl of Dumfries as a replacement for Leifnoreis Castle. The contract was signed on 24th April 1754 and the foundation stone was laid on 18th July 1754. The vaulted basement was completed in August 1755 and the roof was in place by August 1757. The architects were John and Robert Adam, their first major country house commission following the death of their father, William Adam, who was originally to have designed the building. The estimate of £7,979 11s 2d was adhered to within a few pennies! The clerk of works was Robert Neilson and John Mitchell was foreman mason. James Armour, Burns' father-in-law, is believed to have workėd at the erection. Classical in style, the main block measures 95 feet by 65 feet and stands three storeys high plus attic. Though Robert Adam later went on to design much of the furniture he placed in his mansions, at Dumfries House he arranged for items by Sheraton and Chippendale to be sent up from London in 1759. A most sumptious interior was created, as seen in the lower photograph, which is of the Drawing Room. The house was extended, a music room and new dining room being added between the main block and the wings from 1894-1905, the architect being J. Weir Schulz.

AVENUE BRIDGE — Lord Dumfries improved his policies at the same time as Dumfries House was erected. To cross the Lugar he built this particularly grand triple-arched bridge, also the work of John and Robert Adam. Properly known as the Avenue Bridge, it is commonly known as the Adam Bridge from its connection with the famous architects. Across the water is Auchinleck parish, still within Dumfries estate, where a Gothic "Temple" gate was erected in 1760 (designed by John Adam). This caused much wrangling with the Boswells who refused to allow a roadway to be built on the other side.

DOOCOT AND ICEHOUSE — The doocot dates from 1671 making it older than Dumfries House by over 80 years. By a law passed in 1617 only persons owning a certain amount of land were allowed to erect one, and thus it was seen as a status symbol. Rectangular in plan, the doorway is located to the south, over it the arms of the MacDowalls of Freugh, perhaps brought from the castle there. The string-course was used to prevent rats from stealing the eggs. The doocot was restored in 1842. The ice-house was used for storing meat and other foodstuffs during the winter months, it all packed inside with ice.

OLD PARISH CHURCH — This church was erected sometime around 1754 by the Earl of Dumfries, heritor of Old Cumnock Parish. The architects of the building were John and Robert Adam, who were at the time working at Dumfries House. The kirk could accommodate 700 people and in 1822 the internal stairs were removed and replaced by two external flights in order to increase accommodation. These stairs were in great demand for hustings and other public speeches. The wooden shutters were required when the old sport of handball was played in the Square.

OLD MANSE — The former Manse in Robertson Avenue is one of the town's finest old buildings and dates in part from around 1750. The minister at the time was the Revd. Adam Thomson. The building has been extended a number of times since, the oldest part being to the north. The manse and glebe were bought by the council for housing, the manse converted into two flats. The old manse stable, to the rear, has likewise been converted into a dwelling house.

WINSOME WILLIE — William Simson was born at Tenpoundland, near Ochiltree, in 1758 and studied at Glasgow University. He became the schoolmaster at Ochiltree in 1780, transferring to Cumnock in 1788 where his salary was £22 4s 5d in 1803. He wrote a number of poems, including an epistle in verse to Robert Burns who replied with his "Epistle to William Simson" in May 1785. Burns probably visited Simson at Cumnock on occasions, and he called him "Winsome Willie". Simson died in 1815 and his grave, with a verse by A.B. Todd, is to be seen in the old cemetery.

> *I gat your letter, winsome Willie;*
> *Wi' gratefu' heart I thank you brawlie,*
> *Tho' I maun say't, I wad be silly*
> *And unco vain,*
> *Should I believe, my coaxin' billie,*
> *Your flatterin' strain.*

CUMNOCK BURNS CLUB — The Cumnock Burns Club was founded in 1887 and met in the Dumfries Arms. This Burns Supper programme cover dates from 1909, the 150th anniversary of Burns' birth. In the chair that year was Adam Brown Todd, the club's poet laureate. In 1961 the club's annual supper was televised, and has been done so since. The Cumnock Burns Club was not the oldest in the town, the Winsome Willie Burns Club being founded in 1856. Other clubs include the Cumnock Cronies Burns Club, Tam Samson Burns Club, Jolly Beggars Burns Club, and Logangate Burns Club at Logan.

TOWNHEAD STREET — Townhead Street was the main centre in Cumnock for weaving, and these houses are typical of those built by weavers - single-storey, thatched, with two main rooms, one of which had the handloom in it. Some had as many as six looms. At the time of the Statistical Account in 1791 Cumnock had 35 handlooms plus 39 muslin weavers and 7 stocking weavers. By 1811 there were 70 muslin weavers and by the 1830s over 120 looms. The American Civil War and the introduction of power looms led to the decline of the trade in the 1850s until only three weavers worked in 1899.

THE TOONHEID SMIDDY — The smithy in Townhead Street survives in part as Mills' ironmongery shop. This photograph shows the three Merry brothers, John, Harry and Charlie, posing outside. Their father, James Merry, was smith before them, having succeeded his father, Henry Merry, who came to Cumnock in the 1880s from Maybole. On the ground is a large iron ring, used in the manufacture of cart-wheels, rims of which are perched against the wall. It was placed over the wheel and clamped down to the circular stone, with iron loop, whilst the rim was put on. This was known as a Tyring Platform.

DUMFRIES ARMS HOTEL — The Dumfries Arms was originally known as the New Inn or Heid Inn, it being the first inn erected outwith the immediate centre of the village. Dating from the 25th March 1717, it was an important coaching inn and many notable people have stayed there, including Robert Burns and Sir Walter Scott. When the latter visited on 29th June 1817 he wrote in fun, "Old Cumnock, where beds are as hard as a plank, sir." The name of the inn was changed to the Dumfries Arms in 1840. The building looks much the same today, apart from the removal of the tall chimney and the alteration to the porch.

JAMES TAYLOR'S HOUSE — In 1800 James Taylor, inventor of steam navigation and manager of Cumnock Pottery, obtained a 99 year lease of a piece of ground in Ayr Road from Lord Dumfries where he proposed to build a house for himself. The lease stipulated that the house be erected within three years to the value of "10 pounds sterling lease." Taylor's house (now 53 Ayr Road) is claimed by some to be the oldest two storey house in Cumnock. It remained in the family's ownership for a number of years after his death, passing into the ownership of the Murray family in 1908, which family retain it.

CUMNOCK POTTERY — Work commenced at the Pottery at Greenbraehead in 1791, set up by the 6th Earl of Dumfries to produce graphite crucibles. James Taylor was the first manager, remaining until his death in 1825. The pottery lost money until 1812, by which time production had changed to conventional pots. Noted for its "Scotch Motto Ware" the pottery remained in business until 1907. Mottoes, which appeared on everything from candlesticks to milk jugs, included "Help yersel' - dinna be late", "I'm no' greedy but I like a lot", "There's plenty mair in the kitchen" or "Haun roon the poorie." An ink well would be inscribed "We'll be proud tae here frae ye", an egg cup "Tak anither egg", a candlestick "Guid nicht", a bowl "Rax furrit yer haun an help yersel" or a milk jug "Tak a waucht for luck". For a time personalised items of pottery were popular, especially teapots inscribed with the house-wife's name. The lower picture shows a salt container inscribed "Mrs And⩊ Kennedy Cumnock 1892". The oldest known surviving piece of pottery, preserved in the Baird Institute, has on it "William McCroan, Weaver at Chapel, 1801."

VIEW FROM SHANKSTON — This early engraving of Cumnock of around 1850 appeared as the frontispiece of Revd. James Murray's book, *Songs of the Covenant Times*. It views the town from near Shankston, which thatched cottage is seen to the left. The hub of the town can be seen round the spire of the old parish church, with a separate community of houses at Barrhill, to either side of which are the two Barrhill Pit chimneys. The large house in the centre is Broomhill, the other prominent building being the Dumfries Arms, with the Pottery Row extending eastward from it. The chimney of the pottery can be made out behind.

THE TOLL COTTAGE — Taken in 1859, this photograph shows the old Toll Cottage which was situated at the corner of Glaisnock Street and Ayr Road. On the wall are two wooden signs which listed the scale of fees for passage along the turnpike roads, and on the extreme left can be made out part of the actual gate. Though the fees payable are no longer known, they are probably comparable with those paid elsewhere, for example, "For every Horse, or Beast, Drawing any Coach, Barouche, Chariot, Landeau, Chaise, Calash, Chair, Taxed Cart, Hearse, or such other Carriage - 4d."

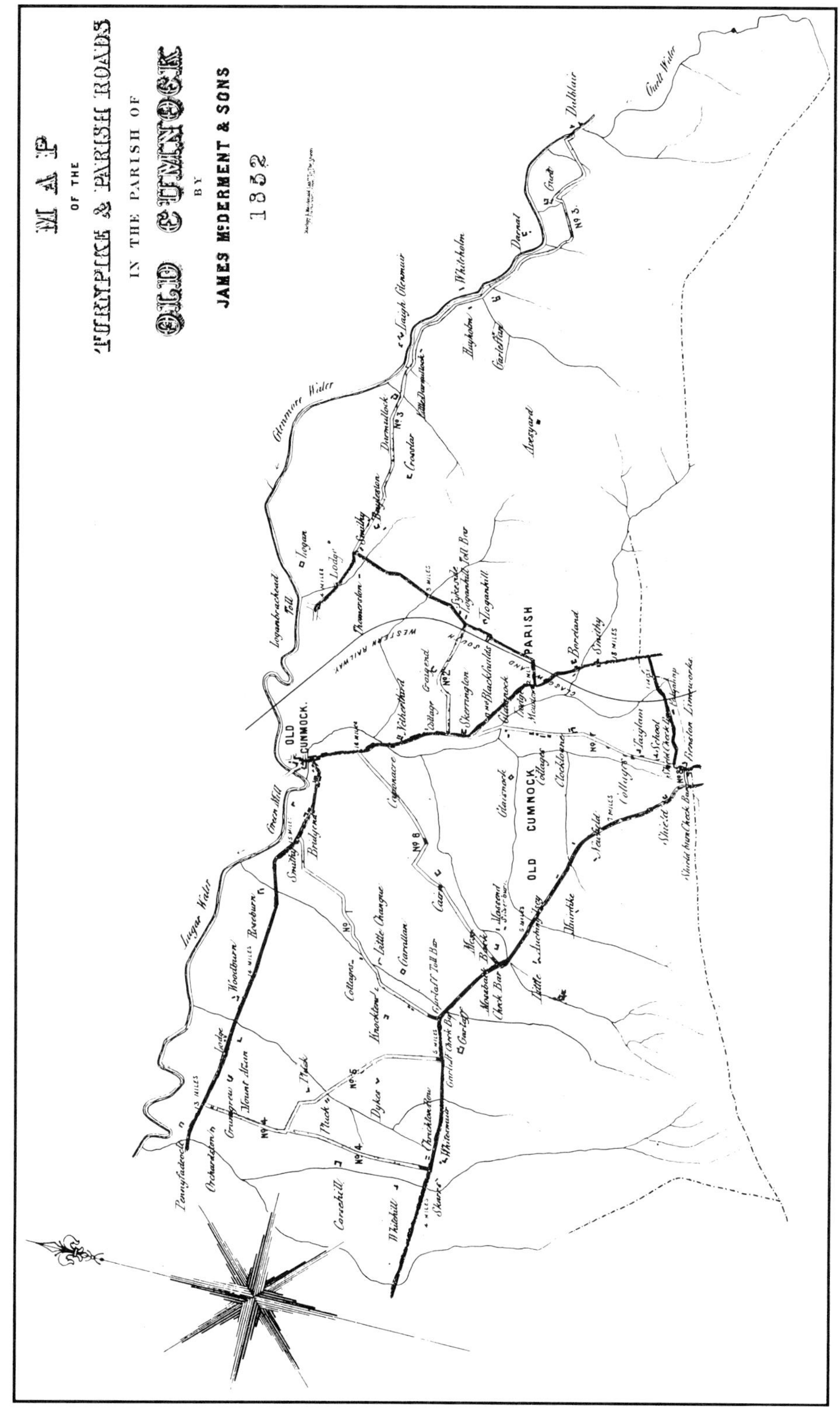

TURNPIKE ROADS — In 1766 and 1774 two Ayrshire Turnpike Acts were passed by parliament. Toll cottages and check-bars were erected at intervals along the roads, and travellers, even if taking a cow to market, had to pay for the privilege of using the roads. This map of the parish of Old Cumnock shows the toll roads in use in 1852. Not shown was the toll located at the junction of Glaisnock Street and Ayr Road, later replaced by tolls at Bridgend and Pottery Row. The tolls on the roads were abolished in 1878, to be replaced by a road assessment, taken over by the County Council in 1889.

LOGAN HOUSE — Logan House dated from the early 19th century and was built on the site of an older building. The estate at one time extended to 3,700 acres but was broken up in the 1920s. One of the most noted owners was Hugh Logan of that Ilk (1739-1802) who was celebrated throughout the country as a wit. A volume of anecdotes, entitled *The Laird of Logan*, many of which were attributed to him, was published in 1854 and went through many editions. The Laird erected a curious pillar at Logan which stood until recently. He squandered his money and had to sell Logan estate in 1798.

GARRALLAN HOUSE — Garrallan was owned by the Campbells until 1676 followed by the Douglas family which became extinct in the male line. Jane Douglas married Hamilton Boswell taking it to that family, who retained it until 1914 when it was sold to the Stevenson's of Changue, the present owners. Dr Patrick Douglas (died 1819) also owned an estate in Jamaica and it was he who offered the job there to Robert Burns in 1786 but which the poet declined. Burns visited Garrallan that year. The house was built in stages, there being datestones, some with arms, of 1660, 1676, 1856, 1868 and 1874.

GLAISNOCK HOUSE — Built around 1833, Glaisnock was designed by James Ingram of Kilmarnock for James Allason, owner at that time. The house has been extended since. The estate was broken up in 1949, the mansion and immediate policies being bought by the county council and opened in 1952 as a junior secondary school. Taking boarders as well as day pupils, the school specialised in rural education and was much beloved of farmers. In 1968 it was upgraded to a four-year school, but it was closed in June 1973. It subsequently became a residential centre for outdoor studies.

HILLSIDE HOUSE — Originally known as Hillside Cottage, this house was erected in 1846 by a Mr Crichton, formerly factor to Lord Bute. His son, Hew, moved to Edinburgh to head Tait and Crichton, Writers to the Signet. His son, James Arthur Crichton, became Sheriff of Lothian and Peebles. The second grandson, Hew Hamilton Crichton tenanted the house until 1906, his spinster sister until 1908. The grounds were noted for its flowers and trees. Attached to it was a conservatory, vinery and greenhouses. In 1909 the house was sold to the parish School Board for £1500 and used for additional classrooms.

VIEWS FROM STEPENDS — One of the traditional locations for viewing Cumnock was from the summit of the old bing at Stepends. This was a relic from the former ironstone mine which stood behind the Congregational Church, disused since 1892. The upper photograph dates from after 1900, when the Crichton spire was built. In the bottom right-hand corner is Stepends House, owned by Robert Lawrence Baird, ironmaster, but at that time leased by Dr John Gilmour Kerr (died 1906). The Parish and Congregational churches are obvious, with Lugar Street between them. Closer inspection reveals a number of tall chimneys, associated with the gasworks and businesses in the Townfoot. The lower photograph is more recent, having been taken in the early 1960s. The town has grown considerably in the intervening years, with Car Road, Netherthird, Craigens and Barshare developments visible. Though a pathway has been created to the summit of the bing, the same view is today even more obscured by the growth of trees.

THE SQUARE — The Square continued to be the hub of Cumnock up until it was pedestrianised, with buses, cars and pedestrians giving it a greater buzz than it currently enjoys. This view dates from between 1900 and 1911 and shows the market cross with a gas lamp on it. Below the Royal Hotel was Carruthers' boot and shoe warehouse. The building on the extreme right was then occupied by Robert Crawford, watchmaker. Next door was Cadam MacClure's confectionery, after whom Caddie's Close was named. Drummond's drapery and MacGeachin's ironmongery are next, followed by Hunter's cycle and ironmongery shop.

HIRING FAIR — It used to be common for farm labourers to be hired or fee'd at bi-annual fairs held in Cumnock. The farmhands would try to find a job which paid more than their last one, and would be bound to that farm for the incoming months. This picture shows such a day in Glaisnock Street. In the middle can be seen a magician entertaining the public, with two policemen in the bottom right corner. Behind is John MacGavin's bakery, with a notice advertising his famed hot pies, to the right Andrew's chemist shop below the Craighead Inn. John Andrew was noted for his "Prize Medal Aerated Waters."

AYR ROAD CORNER — Both of these photographs depict the corner of Ayr Road with Glaisnock Street. Note the dirt roads and cobbled pavements. The upper photograph is taken looking up Munn's Brae towards the old stables of the Dumfries Arms Hotel at Lord Bute's coming of age. Affixed to the gable is the original weather cock from the 1754 parish kirk. When the stables were demolished in 1965 Charles Ancell presented the cock to the Baird Institute. On the left is the Royal Bank, erected in 1866. This bank first opened in the town in 1856 under Andrew White, manager until 1879, followed by Archibald Brakenridge until 1933. The lower photograph was taken around 1890 looking north and shows a temporary ceremonial arch which was erected on special occasions. The figure is at the door of William MacLatchie's house. Next door, where the Co-Op was built, was Jean Ramage's grocery shop. She also sold home-made ginger beer and pop. Left again was Duncan Ballantine's building, erected in 1863. Ballantine and his son ran a printers and stationers here, latterly run by Alexander MacKechnie. Margaret Lindsay had a drapery in the right-hand shop. The light-coloured building had a grocer's and draper's shop, latterly becoming Lipton's.

BANK OF SCOTLAND — The first branch of the Bank of Scotland was opened in Cumnock at the home of Matthew MacKerrow, cloth merchant, in 1838. In 1870 the bank premises shown were erected at the corner of Glaisnock Street and Ayr Road. The architects were J.D. Peddie and C.G.H. Kinnear of Edinburgh, using the neo-baronial style which was then in vogue and which they specialised in. The building was used by the Bank until they moved into their present premises in the new shopping area in Townhead Street, the old bank being used by a printer then solicitor.

The Clydesdale Bank in the Square succeeded the premises at 18-20 the Square, known as Clydesdale House, built in 1846 by the Western Bank of Scotland. Previously there had been a branch of the Ayrshire Banking Company on the same site, set up in 1834. The Royal Bank probably came to Cumnock in 1856 when a fireproof safe was purchased. The present premises were opened ten years later. A National Commercial Bank existed from around 1920, R.D. Hunter being its agent. It was later taken over by the Royal Bank and subsequently closed. The Savings Bank of Glasgow also set up in the town, now the TSB.

CRAWFORD'S TEAROOM — This early photograph shows three waitresses outside what was J. Crawford's dinner and tea room. This was located at the foot of the Pawn Steps, facing onto Bank Lane. The shop was later occupied by Matthew Riggans, butcher, before he got the shop in Bank Lane. Andrew MacCall, better known as "Dusky", then used the building as a fish and chip shop. It was latterly occupied by the Greenan Laundry Company as a dry cleaners. The building is now demolished.

THE GLEBE — This picture depicts the Glebe prior to its acquisition by the council and the erection of houses upon it. At the bottom is the Sandbed Mill, an old establishment, occupied by Alexander Duncan until 1692, and afterwards by the MacGawn family. It latterly became a bakery and was burned down in 1963. Behind is the manse, above it Broomhill House. This was originally the home of William Baird, ironmaster, but was latterly owned by Matthew MacKerrow, banker, who died in 1878. To its left is the old slaughterhouse, erected in 1869 and closed in 1934.

CRAIGHEAD CLOSE — This fairly recent photograph depicts a quaint and rather old corner of the town. Indeed, it is claimed that the oldest surviving building in Cumnock is the one at the end of the close with the arched window, used at that time by Freddie Williams as a bookmakers. It probably dates from the early 18th century. The Craighead Inn on the left, after which the close is named, is also an old building, reputedly haunted in the attic, and dating perhaps from before 1722 when a lease was drawn up for the annual payment of £21 plus two hens and two loads of coal.

OLD PARISH CHURCH — This magnificent building was erected between 1863 and 1867 in the Gothic style to the plans of James Maitland Wardrop of Edinburgh. Yellow sandstone from Coalburn, near New Cumnock, was used. The cost of construction was £6227 14s 8d though the proposed spire was not built, its intended location over the clock capped off. On the north side of the church is a Bute vault, with a gallery for the Marquis's use inside the nave. There are some good examples of stained glasswork, some by Ballantyne from 1867, one window signed A.L. Moore, London.

INTERIOR OF OLD KIRK — This view shows the ornate interior of the parish church in the Square, looking south. As can be seen the pulpit was formerly placed centrally in front of a pipe organ. This was removed in 1966 at the time of the church building's centenary and a mosaic formed on the wall behind.

LADY BUTE'S HOSPITAL — The Bute Hospital was the gift of Lady Bute in 1882. Staffed by trained nurses from the Sisters of the Sacred Heart, the hospital had ten beds and three cots. Used for all types of general medical work, it was often required to treat victims of mining accidents. After 1920 a committee ran the hospital until 1950 and the formation of the health service, at which time it was closed. It later became a convent but was demolished and replaced by the Murray Court houses.

BELL TREE — When the old parish church was demolished in 1864 to make way for the present kirk the old bell was removed from the spire and temporarily hung on an old tree in The Strand. It continued in use, being rung daily at 5:30 am and 8:00 pm and on Sundays by the bellman, Hugh MacLellan. However, when the kirk was finished a new bell had been donated, making the old bell redundant. It hung on the bell tree for eight years, being later housed in a small belfry in the public school, as shown. Dating from 1697, the ornate bell was cast by Quirinus de Visscher of Rotterdam.

THE PUBLIC SCHOOL — Old Cumnock Public School was erected in 1875 (foundation stone laid 19th August) at a cost of £2700 and officially opened on 6th October 1876. The architect employed was R.S. Ingram, using Mid-pointed Gothic with depressed arches. It is thought he based the school on a design by William Lambie Moffat. When opened at first there were joint headmasters, David Scott and Robert Brown, the latter continuing after Mr Scott's retiral in 1882 until 1899. John Dick succeeded, followed by Andrew Martin and John Edgar, the latter an ex-provost. The building was demolished around 1974.

CLASS PHOTOGRAPH — Taken early this century, this picture was a class photograph taken at the Public School on Barrhill Road. Classes were generally larger in those days, here numbering 42, arranged round their teacher. Fashions in schoolwear have changed, boys wearing wide starched collars and girls dressed in pinafores or smocks.

UNITED PRESBYTERIAN CHURCH — Cumnock Associate Church (Burgher) was built in 1831 on the site of the earlier 1775 church at a cost of £876 11s. Tradesmen included Andrew Murdoch and J Nimmo, masons, David Kier, slater, William Black and William MacLetchie, wrights, Hugh Maitlen, plasterer and William Thomson, plumber. It had room for 851 worshippers. The first minister (in the old church) was Revd. James Hall, ordained at the age of 20. He was followed by Revd. David Wilson and Revd. Robert Brown, who died in 1847. In the same year it became United Presbyterian, with Matthew Dickie as minister. A hall, vestry and session house was added to the rear in 1904, a pipe organ installed internally. In 1900 the U.P. and Free churches merged nationally, creating the United Free Church of Scotland, of which this became one, styled Cumnock West U.F. Church. The town then had two U.F. churches, the other being the Crichton Memorial. Both of these became parish churches in 1929. The old West Kirk is a particularly fine example of a Scots "box kirk" and is the oldest church building in the town. In 1923 Revd. Hugh MacKniven Agnew wrote a history of the church to celebrate its 150th anniversary.

THE WEST KIRK — In 1868 the United Presbyterian Church demolished the old manse in Auchinleck Road and had a new building erected on the same site. The old manse, which was erected around 1780, is shown at the foot of the opposite page, and is the one to which Robert Burns paid a visit. In 1788 the session paid the minister £70 per annum, with manse, and the farmer members agreed to supply the use of a horse, except in seedtime and harvest. It was often required, for the minister's flock lived up to 12 miles away. The new manse building survives, shown above as it looks today. Costing £930 to build, £200 of this was granted by the Manse Board. The manse was sold off in 1949 and became known as Ferguslea and in more recent years as Cameron House, catering for tourists as a bed and breakfast establishment. The lower picture shows the Kirk Session members of the now United Free church in 1923, seated in front of the manse door. In September 1949 the West Church and the Crichton Memorial Church merged, using the latter building which was renamed the Crichton West Church. The West Kirk was sold to the county council for use as a store.

OLD CUMNOCK STATION — With the coming of the railway in 1850 a station was created on the Barr Hill, opening on 20th May that year. With the line extended to link with that from Dumfries, the Glasgow, Paisley, Kilmarnock and Ayr Railway Company merged with the Glasgow, Dumfries and Carlisle Railway Company to form the Glasgow and South-Western on 28th October 1850. Both of these photographs show the Cumnock side of the railway, with the stationmaster's house. The station here was closed with most others on the line in the Beeching Cuts of 6th December 1965. A second station existed in the town, called Cumnock New Station. This was on the Ayr and Cumnock line and was located where George McTurk Court now stands. This station was opened in 1874, passenger services withdrawn in 1951 and the line closed and lifted in 1964.

FREE CHURCH — At the Disruption in 1843 the Revd. Ninian Bannatyne and many of his congregation left the parish kirk and formed a Free Church. Within a short period of time they built this church building in Ayr Road, complete with school and manse, opened for worship in October 1843. It remained in use until the summer of 1896 when it was demolished and work commenced on the new church, shown below. Bannatyne died in 1874, followed by Revd. Alexander Adamson and Revd. John Warrick, ordained on 22nd February 1883. It was he who wrote the *History of Old Cumnock*, published in 1899.

CRICHTON MEMORIAL CHURCH — Erected between 1896-1899, this large church was paid for by Miss Crichton of Hillside in memory of her father, Hew Crichton, and her brother, Sheriff James Crichton, both of whom died in 1892. English Gothic in style, the architect was David Menzies of Edinburgh. The building can seat 500 and the spire stands 140 feet tall. Originally a Free Church, it became a United Free Church in 1900 and a Church of Scotland in 1929. It has been known as Crichton West since 1949. This attractive photograph depicts the church from the rear, seen from Elbow Lane.

MACCARTNEY'S ENGINEERING WORKS — George MacCartney established his business at Clockclownie farm in 1812 but in 1832 moved to this site at Greenholm, employing six men and a blacksmith. The company became well-known for its engineering output which included threshing machines, mill equipment and even bridge frameworks. At one time a hundred threshing mills were made and sold each year at around £80 each. Following the visit of Kirkpatrick MacMillan in 1842 MacCartney made a copy of the first ever bicycle. George MacCartney died unmarried in 1868 aged 78 and was buried in Ochiltree. The business was carried on by others as George MacCartney and Company, being taken over by Charles and Andrew Taylor in 1901. They diversified into electrical switchgear but the factory closed in 1933 during the years of depression. The upper photograph shows the works, on the right-hand side of the bridge, a particularly fine example of a mid 19th century factory, formerly powered by water from a dam across the Glaisnock. The lower photograph shows some of the employees in 1923 complete with samples of their work. Back left to right: Taylor, Milne, Corbett, Simpson, Dalziel and Marshall. Front: Pyle, Miller, Kennedy, Hodge, Duncan, Finn and Cooper.

NEW BLACKFAULD SQUARE — Shown here are the houses at New Blackfauld Square (or Clocklochar) which stood to the east of the present Craigens houses, the site now occupied by Almar cottage. Having six houses, the square, actually E shaped, dates from before 1860, being shown on the 6" Ordnance Survey Map of that time. It was owned by the Marquis of Bute. The house on the extreme left was occupied by Thomas Gibson who worked on the railways. There was a smithy here, worked in 1900 by Samuel MacKendrick and Hector Walker. Old Blackfauld stood next to the railway, across from Loganhill, and south of the toll.

SKARES ROWS — William Baird & Co. built 118 houses in three rows at Skares to house their miners, employed in the local pits. The houses were all two apartment dwellings, though the Front Row of 42 houses had the additional luxury of a scullery and back door! The rent for these houses was £5 per annum, exclusive of rates. Every five houses had a dry-closet and every eight a wash-house. The Middle Row had 40 houses, the kitchens of which measured 14 feet by 11, the other room 10 feet square. The Back Row had 36 houses. The rows were cleared of people from 1949 onwards and later demolished.

BANK VIADUCT — The railway to Cumnock was opened on 20th May 1850 by the Glasgow, Paisley, Kilmarnock and Ayr Railway Company, two years after it had reached Auchinleck. The Bank Viaduct was one of the great feats of engineering on this line, thirteen arches crossing the glen, the highest of which stands 175 feet above the Lugar Water. The engineer of the bridge was John Miller, of Miller and Grainger of Edinburgh, and hundreds of Irish navvies and colonials were employed as labourers. The viaduct is still used by the Glasgow to Dumfries railway.

GLEN LUGAR QUARRIES — Many of the early buildings in Cumnock were constructed from stone taken from the quarries in Glen Lugar. Dumfries House and the Bank Viaduct, seen here in the background, were certainly built of stone quarried here. When Dumfries House was built the stone was dragged by oxen to the site, one of the last times cattle were used for such a purpose. The part of the quarry shown here, long abandoned, was located on the Roadinghead side of the river, where once two ironstone pits worked. Another quarry existed at the end of the Mote Hill, and a third nearer Longhouse, known as Logan Quarry.

GLAISNOCK VIADUCT — In 1872 the Glasgow and South Western Railway Company built a second railway line through Cumnock, called the Ayr and Cumnock branch line. Across the Glaisnock a viaduct of thirteen arches was erected, the tallest arch being 75 feet above the level of the water. Many Irish navvies were used in the construction of the bridge, and the lower photograph shows work at an early stage, with the wooden scaffold used to support the grabs for hauling up the sandstone blocks. Note the rough wooden ladder used to climb onto the upper platform. The viaduct is sometimes known as the Deil Stone Viaduct, from the Deil Stane, a large boulder which, if run round a number of times, would result in Auld Nick's appearance! His hoofprints were reputedly to be seen on the stone. The viaduct was closed to trains in 1964 and converted to a pathway. Through the arch is seen Netherthird farm.

RIVERSIDE HOUSE — This sizeable house, located in Lugar Street, dates in part from the late 18th century (the front half). The extension to the rear was added in the mid 19th century. It was owned by the Gray family, James Gray being a coalmaster and the first chairman of Cumnock Parish Council from 1895 until his death, on 25th February 1904 at the age of 81. Gray Street was named after him.

MILLBANK HOUSE — Millbank dates from shortly after 1860, being built on a corner of the Glebe. By 1900 it was owned by James Morrison of Blackbush Cottage, Ochiltree, but tenanted by Hugh Climie, flesher in the town. It later became the home of the Livingstone family, grocers in Lugar Street. In 1931 the house was sold to Cumnock District Council who used it as their headquarters, meeting in a room upstairs. There is a registry office within. In 1975, at regionalisation, the house passed to Strathclyde Regional Council as their Cumnock Local Office.

CONGREGATIONAL CHURCH — In 1882 the Congregationalists built themselves a new church across the Lugar Bridge in what was then still part of Auchinleck parish. The "neat little Gothic structure," designed by John Murdoch of Ayr, was opened on Sunday 18th February 1883 "free of debt," having cost £1600 to build. Built to seat 400, at a later date a manse and halls were added. Only five ministers have served here since then, William Mathieson, Mark Robson, James Drife, William Thomson and Matthew Sullivan.

BAPTIST CHURCH — The Baptist Church was erected in 1887 on the Barrhill with seating for 200. The first Baptists in the district arrived in 1875 to Gasswater and employed their first minister the year following. They occupied various buildings, including the parish school before the present church was built. Because of the sloping site, a small hall is located below the kirk. A porch was added to the front in the 1970s. The Baptists had many short ministries for decades, and a fluctuating membership, varying from 53 in 1926 to around 100 in 1966.

ROYAL HOTEL — The present hotel building, facing up Glaisnock Street, was erected around 1892 by R.J. Barrowman, the proprietor. The earlier block, in the Square, is of mid 19th century date. For some years it was known as the Hotel Royal, and boasted "spacious Dining, Drawing, Reading, Smoking and Billiard Room, with numerous Single and Double Bedrooms." In 1956 the hotel was bought by Stevenson's Dairy Farms, the present proprietors. This view from Glaisnock Street shows the building when George MacMillan had his bookshop below the hotel.

MARIO LUNI'S — This building at the corner of Ayr Road was erected in 1873 on the site of the toll. It formerly had two shops on the ground floor, leased at times by Mackervail's, Hugh Lorimer's clothing shop, R. Craig then James Millar's millinery, and Mary Miller's Confectionery. From before 1915 until the building was demolished it was the premises of Mario then Ernesto Luni, whose ice-cream was famous. On one occasion a tank descending Glaisnock Street failed to take the corner and smashed through the wall. Mario Luni is reputed to have held up his hands and said, "No ice-da creamy today!"

THE TOWNHEAD — This postcard above, of about 1885 depicts the foot of Townhead Street. The thatched cottage on the left was occupied by Mrs Lennox, dressmaker, who had the front white-washed every week. Muir's building stood behind. The building with its gable facing the camera was occupied by Andrew MacMillan, barber, the one below the lamp being Frank Digby's lodging house. The dark building on the extreme right was Mathieson's shoe shop, latterly a butcher's. The small building was "Batchy" Smith's bakery, with Mrs MacSherrie's children's clothes shop projecting into the street.

THE SQUARE — This photograph of the Square dates from before 1892 when the Royal Hotel extension was built. Before then the site was occupied by the shops seen here. That to the left was occupied by James Purdie, saddler and harness maker. Previously it had been occupied by Hugh Climie, butcher, whose business survives today in Glaisnock Street. To the right was Carruthers' boot and shoe warehouse, firstly David Carruthers followed by John, provost for a time. The Carruthers' were successors to David Kennedy.

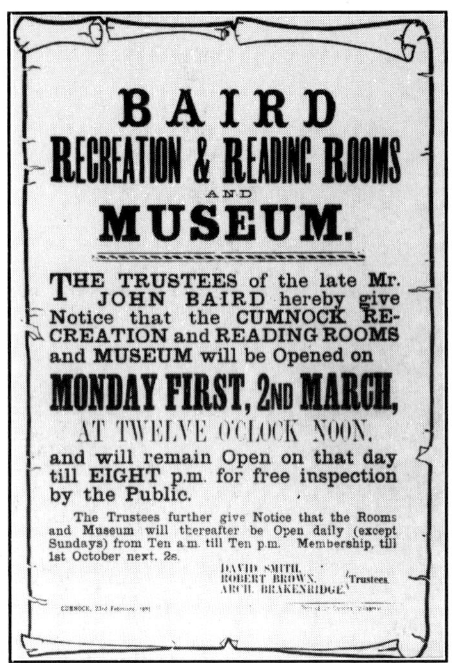

BAIRD INSTITUTE — John Baird, shown top right, draper and architect, died unmarried on 27th July 1888 aged 76 and is buried in the old cemetery. He was the son of David Baird, landlord of the Tup Inn, and grew up with an interest in literature, photography, cabinet-making and lepidoptery. He served on the council from 1874-77. A number of houses in the town were designed by Baird, such as Muirfield in Glaisnock Street. Baird left most of his money to establish a public institute and museum which was erected adjacent to his house and drapery shop in Lugar Street. The lower photograph shows some of the tradesmen involved.

The Baird Institute cost £2250 to erect and was designed by Robert Samson Ingram in a neo-baronial style, part of the original plans being shown below. The official opening was performed by Mrs Brakenridge, wife of the Town Clerk, on Monday 2nd March 1891. A copy of the original poster announcing the opening is depicted on the preceding page. Archibald Brakenridge, Robert Brown and David Smith were the original three trustees. A small fee was payable by those who wished to use the facilities. Within were a reading room, recreation room, and museum room, many of the artefacts being from Baird's own collection. The building was run by the Baird Trustees until 1972 when it was handed over to the Burgh. The building was restored and in 1980 was reopened by Cumnock and Doon Valley District Council, the library service operating the museum with changing exhibitions and various groups meeting in the hall.

ANDREW CARNEGIE'S VISIT — Andrew Carnegie, the lad born in Dunfermline who became the world's richest man, visited Cumnock on two occasions, this photograph showing him on the second as he passed along Ayr Road. He is seen on the carriage, holding the reins, with Mrs Carnegie at his side. He had just left the Dumfries Arms where he had invited A.B. Todd to meet him. Also in the photograph is James Murray, landlord at the hotel, and David Scott, headmaster at the school.

AYR ROAD — This view shows Ayr Road early this century. On the right was Jean MacCubbin's millinery. The cyclists are outside the old Post Office, which existed here from 1880 until 1911, run by George Stoddart, postmaster. Previously the office had been in the Square. Next door was Mrs Lennox's clothes shop, it and the post office becoming A.F. Borland's ironmongery. The building next door, at this time occupied by David Murray, draper, was demolished and the Masonic Lodge erected on the site. The Parish Council offices were in the centre shop erected by the Crichtons, with R.D. Hunter next door.

VICTORIA FOUNTAIN — To commemorate the Diamond Jubilee of Queen Victoria's reign this fountain was erected in the Square on the east side of the kirk in 1898. Made of pink granite, with two drinking spouts, it was topped by an incandescent gas lamp. In 1928, due to increasing traffic in the Square, it was removed to the circle at Gemmell Avenue and virtually forgotten about by the residents of the burgh.

OPENING OF THE POST OFFICE — The first post office in Cumnock was located in Lugar Street and it was there in 1910 the present premises were built, George Stoddart continuing as postmaster until his death in 1917. A telephone exchange was added in 1912. This picture was taken at the official opening with, seated, left to right: R Cunningham, J Hume, Miss Murdoch, T Pollock, D Smith, Mrs Aird, Miss Crichton, J O'Neil, R Houston, A Brakenridge, J Bingham, J Andrew, J Crawford and Revd. Mathieson, who has moved. Standing: A Miller, J Morrison, W Morrison, M Taylor, J Fleming, Revd. Warrick, Dr Armitage, -?-, W MacNaughton, Mr Small, Mrs Livingstone, AB Todd, J Livingstone, Mr Lidbury, -?-, G Stoddart, J Richmond, -?-, R Livingstone, Miss Stoddart, Miss Gibson, J Samson, Dr MacQueen, Revd. MacDonald, R Hope, D White, -?-, Fr Meagher, J Yates, M Jamieson and R Samson.

THE CRUCIFIX — The marble crucifix was erected next to the Nest Burn by John, 3rd Marquis of Bute, near the spot where he was converted to Roman Catholicism on 9th October 1900. This conversion was regarded as a great coup for Rome and it is said to have inspired *Lothair* by Benjamin Disraeli. Over Christ's head are the letters INRI (Jesus of Nazareth, King of the Jews), below his feet the motto Thy Wounds are my Merits. The inscription reads: HOEC SACROSANCTA IMAGO JVSSV JOANNIS MARCHIONIS III BOTHÆ ERECTA EST PROPE LOCVM VBI IPSE ANIMAM DEO REDDIDIT DIE IX OCTOBR ANN MDCCCC.

BUTE CELEBRATIONS — Parades through the town were at one time fairly common to celebrate various notable events in the life of the Bute family. Comings of Age, Weddings, and Birthdays have all been celebrated with street processions. This photograph shows the Square decorated with flags and bunting at the turn of the century to "Welcome Hame" Lord Bute. It was taken in 1902 when the 4th Marquis became of age and when he came to the town to receive an address from the council.

TOWN HALL — Built by subscription, work on the Town Hall commenced in 1883 on a site donated by the Marquis of Bute. On 7th June 1885 the hall was declared open but it took until 1895 to pay off the loan. The architect was R.S. Ingram and the building contained two halls, the Lesser Hall located over the council chambers. Many meetings and concerts have taken place in the building, and it has been a noted venue for dances. In 1913 it was used for showing films and the first bingo nights were held in 1957. A fire damaged part of the building in 1983 but it was subsequently restored.

KEIR HARDIE'S BUST — The National Keir Hardie Committee commissioned the Queen's Sculptor in Scotland, Benno Schotz, to create a bronze bust of Keir Hardie. Three copies of this were made, one presented to Merthyr Tydfil in Wales (where he was MP), one to the Houses of Parliament, and this one erected in Cumnock. The bust was presented to the burgh by William Stewart and accepted by Nan Hardie Hughes, Keir Hardie's daughter and provost at the time. The memorial was unveiled in August 1939. Plans for a complete statue in 1916 came to nought.

ST JOHN'S R.C. CHURCH— The 3rd Marquis of Bute gave financial assistance towards the erection of a chapel in Cumnock, the Roman Catholics previously worshipping at Birnieknowe. Lord Bute employed William Burges to design the building, in Early Decorated style, he being noted for his work at Cardiff Castle and Cork Cathedral. Like the parish kirk, the intended tower was not erected. In 1885 it was the first church in the country to install electricity using a generator.

The long apse has painted boards on the ceiling by J.F. Bentley and stained glass by Westlake. The nave roof has unusual king-posts. The manse of St. John's Roman Catholic Church was erected in 1913 for Revd. Martin Meaghar, priest from 1906 until 1936, later canonised, and after whom Meaghar Court was named in 1971. The architect of the house was Reginald Fairlie, a noted Scots architect and successor to Sir Robert Lorimer. The building was actually a mirror image of the presbytery erected simultaneously at Troon Our Lady of the Assumption and St. Meddan's R.C. Church, though the Troon house was built of dressed masonry, the Cumnock one harled. The bottom left photograph shows the high altar within St John's church. Located at the south end of the nave, the chancel lies behind. The stained glass windows date from 1884 and were the work of N.J. Westlake. He also designed the Bute window which dates from 1883 and which was erected to John, Lord Bute, by a grateful congregation. It depicts St Ninian over the Bute arms. The altar, font, tabernacle plinth and pulpit were replaced in the 1960s with modern ones carved from white Creetown granite.

JAMES KEIR HARDIE — Keir Hardie was the illegitimate son of a farm servant, born at Legbranock (Lanarkshire) on 15th August 1856. He came to Cumnock in 1879 as secretary of the Ayrshire Miners' Association, leading them in the strike of 1881 but later dismissed. From 1882-86 he was editor of the *Cumnock News*. In 1886 he became secretary of the Ayrshire Miners' Union and on 26th August 1888 founded the Scottish Labour Party. He was elected member of Parliament in 1892, representing West Ham until 1895. In 1900 he was re-elected as MP for Merthyr Tydfil, retaining it until his death on 16th September 1915.

LOCHNORRIS — James Keir Hardie built this house for himself in 1891. The cost of construction was £600 which he borrowed. To the rear of the house, overlooking the Lugar Water, he built a small summer house where he wrote many of his parliamentary speeches. After Keir Hardie's death the house passed to his daughter and son-in-law, Emlyn Hughes MP, whose family retained it until 1982. At one time there were plans to create a museum in the house but this did not come to fruition.

THE HIGHER GRADE SCHOOL — Hillside House was put up for sale by the Crichton family in 1909 and was purchased by the School Board of Old Cumnock parish for £1500. The postcard above shows how it was partially converted for school use, being opened in 1911. The 143 Higher Grade pupils were ceremoniously marched across the road to their sumptuous new accommodation. This extension again became insufficient to accommodate the pupils, and work commenced on an extension to the right. The lower picture shows some of the Higher Grade pupils at the front door of the school.

MIDDLE STAGES — This photograph shows the former Cumnock Academy in its middle stage of formation, with the new wing added to the converted Hillside House. The rector at the time was Andrew Martin, successor to John Dick. By 1948 Cumnock Academy was the largest school in Ayrshire with a roll of 1443.

OLD ACADEMY — The school building on the right was opened on 31st October 1926 by ex-Provost Thomas Hunter and in December 1927 was renamed Cumnock Academy. The building was much-needed, and contained twelve classrooms, gymnasium and a small swimming pool, located in the centre of the building. The roll at this time was 900. This view shows the school after Hillside House was demolished, and before the east wing was opened in September 1939.

MASONIC LODGE — The Masonic Lodge in Cumnock was founded on 7th August 1809 with the name St Barnabas, Number 230. In 1911-12 they erected a Temple in Ayr Road, under the guidance of the presiding officer, John Hume. The architect was William Cowie of Ayr. The lower floor had a kitchen, smoking room, and entrance hall, the main meeting hall, committee room and tyler's room on the first floor. The hall was used by the lodge, and also the Royal Arch (1909) and Eastern Star (1903) chapters, for over 60 years, it now being converted to flats, the Masons meeting elsewhere.

THE BOER WAR — In 1899 war broke out in South Africa when the Boers demanded independence. It lasted until 1902, Lord Kitchener winning for Britain, but promising to restore an independent government. Eighteen Cumnockians took part in the war, mostly with the Ayrshire Yeomanry, and on their return the Revd. John Warrick published a sermon on the victory, entitled *Bow in the Cloud*. Back left to right: W Ogilvie, H Meikle, A Montgomery, J Park, H Brown. Middle: W MacMillan, H Murdoch, J Armstrong, W Montgomery, D Tear, W Bruges. Front: D MacLanachan, J Murray, W MacLanachan, JD Boswell, J Macartney, J Sloan and J MacDonald.

rails which formerly ran up the Barrhill. Between them was a strip of softer ground, this helping the horses to pull the carts up the steep brae when the surface of the road in general was slippy. Behind the high wall on the right was the garden of Hillside House, now Greenmill school. The lower photograph was taken in the field between Dumfries House Mains and the water cistern. In the distance is the Stairhill Mount, a circular wood, with Dettingen and Bland's mounts, planted to commemorate the Earl of Stair's involvement at the Battle of Dettingen in 1743. The water cistern is located in the small clump of trees on the right. The water for the ''big house'' still passes through it, being piped from Milzeoch farm.

HOLMHEAD HOSPITAL — The first proposals for a fever hospital in Cumnock were made in 1893 by the County Council, but there was considerable wrangling over the proposed location - the town council and others objecting to the proposed Barrhill site, adjacent to the slaughter-house. At length, in 1898, the Marquis of Bute allowed it to be built on his ground at Holmhead. Around half a century later, when cases of tuberculosis and infectious diseases became rare, it was converted to a geriatric hospital.

PICTURE HOUSE — The Picture House was opened in 1913 when the film Monte Cristo was shown to a packed hall. The patrons could choose from the pit or balcony for viewing and there were almost 1000 seats. Films were shown nightly, with two houses on Mondays and Saturdays, the latter day also having a matinee. The cinema was operated by Cumnock Picture House Ltd and the first manager was Mr Frame. Vaudeville (theatrical) acts were performed for a time. The Picture House was later converted to a Bingo Hall, and as such continues.

WOODROAD PARK — 25 acres of the Templand were acquired in 1935 for £500 and a park created, the swimming pool being the main feature. Other facilities included tennis, putting, and playing fields. Ground at Stepends Bing was donated to the burgh in 1937 by Lady Talbot de Malahide of Auchinleck. After the War an open-air dance floor was created. In 1951 the Round Table donated a children's playpark and a bridge to the Glebe was erected in 1953. A camping site was established, and the park became a popular resort for tourists. Many trips come to the park, and it was popular for cyclists' rallies.

TOWNHEAD THISTLE F.C. — A number of football teams existed in Cumnock prior to the Juniors, including Cumnock Thistle, Cumnock Celtic, Cumnock Craigbank, Springbank, Glaisnock Lads and Townhead Thistle. From these teams a Cumnock Select was picked in 1904 which played Glasgow Rangers at New Station Park in a charity match. Rangers won 4-1. This photograph shows the committee and players of Townhead Thistle. The players are: Back Row, left to right: T. Smith, Leslie Reid, Andy MacCall, Jock Boyd, Willie MacCall, Andy Stillie. Front Row: Jimmy White, Willie Jackson, Sam Nicol, Alan MacCall and Ticky Orr.

SWIMMING POOL — The Swimming Pool in the Woodroad Park was opened in June 1936 by Provost Nan Hardie Hughes in front of 2,500 spectators. It had cost £5,500 to build, but originally was opposed to by many of the residents. At length a vote was taken, the "fors" winning 404 to 332. The upper photograph shows work on the pool at an early stage, the hole dug by hand and the excess earth carried away by horse and cart. The pool measures 100 feet by 45 feet with a change in depth from three to ten feet, the deeper end having various diving boards. The pool, though open-air, has heated water and was regarded as one of the finest open-air pools in the country. In winter the pool was often covered and open-air dances held. Two swimming clubs were formed, the Cumnock Amateur Swimming Club and the Cumnock and District Miners' A.S.C., both of which merged in 1963 to form Cumnock Dolphin A.S.C. The pool opens in the summer months each year, the first person to reach the water each year being traditionally awarded a free season ticket.

CARNIVAL IN GLAISNOCK STREET — This picture shows lower Glaisnock Street at one of the early carnivals. Few events today seem to merit such an amount of decoration. On the left is the Temperance Hotel, run by Mrs Pollock, below it Kay the chemist and Mrs Neal's sweet and fruit shop, latterly Nicol's. The Buck's Head Inn was originally owned by James Bain, latterly Alexander MacKechnie, and is now the Glaisnock Inn. On 10th June 1833 a meeting of local farmers was being held inside to discuss actions against poachers. They were constantly disturbed by poachers at the bar, so much so that David Reid was accidentally shot. He had arrived late for the meeting.

THE TOON FIT — Seen from the Tanyard, this picture shows the Townfoot or lower Tower Street prior to the demolitions which have left a virtually building-free street. The low thatched cottage on the right was Sarah Druggan's fish and chip shop, much beloved by the townsfolk. The pram is sitting in front of William MacKerrow's grocery and sweet shop. To the right of the van was Galbraith's shop. Behind it was originally Riggans' butcher shop, latterly Andrew MacCall's fish and chip shop then the Greenan Laundry. All these buildings were demolished in the mid 1960s.

THE TOON HEID — Viewed from Glaisnock Street, this picture shows the entrance to Townhead Street. The building on the left is the Craighead inn, with the lower shop occupied by James Davidson, saddler, who went into it after Andrew the chemist. It was later Mrs Lees china shop and is now part of the inn. James Moodie was a grocer, his shop latterly becoming Tom MacCaughie's fish shop. On the right is MacCubbin's grocery with Alexander White's drapery above. Between the two is Blackwood and Veitch's butcher shop and the double-storey Castlehill Building behind.

LUGAR STREET — Apart from the two buildings on the right, this view has changed little. Behind the bushes is Riverside House, with Kilnholm Place sticking out into the street. Jenny Tear's pub, the Tup Inn, is behind it, the left hand part being originally a home bakery. Across the road is the Post Office and Gibb's Printery. The double storey building on the right hand side of the Tanyard entrance was the Jeannie or Jenny House, latterly occupied as a house by Hugh Lorimer, author of *A Corner of Old Strathclyde*.

ADAM BROWN TODD — Adam Brown Todd was born at Craighall, near Mauchline, on 6th February 1822, a crofter's fourteenth child. He later moved to Barrshouse, near Sorn, in which village he was educated. After a number of years employed on farms and at a tileworks, he became editor of the *Cumnock Express* in 1863, setting up home in the town. He built Breezyhill in Glaisnock Street, shown in the lower photograph. Todd wrote many poems, *The Hermit of Westmorland, and Other Poems* being published in 1846, and two other volumes in 1876 and 1880. He wrote two books on the Covenanters - *Homes, Haunts and Battlefields of the Covenanters* in 1888 and *Covenanting Pilgrimages and Studies* in 1911. His *Poetical Works and Autobiography* appeared in 1906. Todd was an active member of Cumnock society, being a councillor and adversary of Keir Hardie. In 1903 he was given a public luncheon at the Dumfries Arms in his honour. He died in 1915 aged 93 and was buried in the new cemetery. One of his kinsmen, Revd. Sir Garfield Todd, was a missionary who became prime minister of Northern Rhodesia.

JOHN SMITH — A noted geologist and antiquarian, John Smith was born at Clarkston, near Airdrie. He trained as a civil and mining engineer, being employed by William Baird firstly at Lugar Ironworks followed by the Eglinton Ironworks at Kilwinning. He died there on 30th November 1930 aged 86, but was buried in Cumnock's old cemetery. Smith wrote many articles on geology and archaeology for various society journals, but is best remembered for his books, *Prehistoric Man in Ayrshire* (1895) and *Botany of Ayrshire* (1896).

JIMMY OSBORNE — A number of characters have lived in or visited Cumnock over the years, and Jimmy Osborne was one of them. He travelled about the town selling firewood, carrying it on his barrow. On it were the words "James Osborne - Wood Merchant" neatly printed on the handles. Wullie Collins lived in Waterside Row but as both his parents died in bed he preferred to lie in a hole in the floor of his house. He died in 1915 aged 74.

CUMNOCK QUOITING CLUB — The game of quoits was at one time very popular in mining communities. It used circular rings of iron, quite heavy in weight which were thrown at a peg in a clay park, the nearest quoit winning, much the same as in bowls or curling. The oldest park for the game was located in the Townhead, and latterly several inns had their own pitches. This medal was presented by Cumnock Quoiting Club in 1862.

THE ROARING GAME — Curling was played in the parish for centuries though by 1915 it had "suffered with the changed conditions of modern life." The Flush at Townhead was used for many years as a rink, but proved to be unsatisfactory. A good rink was created at Woodhead, on Dumfries estate, but was too distant from the town. Lord Bute granted the Cumnock Curlers a field off Ayr Road in 1905 where a large pond was made but which had difficulties holding water. There were even plans to tarmac the bottom. Indoor rinks killed the sport off locally, though the club was reformed in 1949.

THE RAMBLERS — Cumnock has a long association with the bicycle. A type of wooden horse was made by John Murdoch, the gas-engineer's father, which he used to travel from Bello Mill to Cumnock. Kirkpatrick MacMillan gave the first public demonstration of his cycle on 6th June 1842 by freewheeling down MacKinlay's Brae (Glaisnock Street) with his feet on the handlebars! A Cumnock Cycling Club existed at an early date, the above photograph depicting the members outside the Town Hall at a fancy dress dance. The Cumnock Ramblers Cycling Club was formed in the 1920's, originally as a rambling club, hence the name, but gradually the cycling side became more important. The Ramblers were a popular club,  organising the renowned Cumnock Rally to which cyclists from all over the west of Scotland flocked. The photograph below, dating from the 1930s, shows most of the members: Back Left to Right: Johnny Ramsay, Willie Ronald, "Dainty" Dick, Mick Ogilvie, John Ferguson (proprietor of Sun Inn), Pat Reid Senior, Johnny Dunsmuir, Adam Stein, Jim Meikle. Middle Row: Davie Ronald, Frank MacCormick, Sam Hogg, Pat Reid Junior, Willie, Jim and George Milligan. Front Row: Davie Kyle, Jim Pooley, Alex Dillon, Jimmy Kyle, Jimmy Milgrew and Johnny Dillon.

ALL SAINTS CHURCH — All Saints Church stood across the road from Glaisnock House gates and was associated with that mansion. The photograph shows the church's Sunday School on a trip to Glaisnock House, posing on the front steps, in 1911. All Saints Church was originally Episcopalian in denomination but for a number of years had services conducted by Revd. William Mathieson, minister of the Congregational Church. The church has long-since been demolished.

ST ANDREW'S U.F. CHURCH — With the reunion of the United Free and Church of Scotland in 1929 some adherents of the U.F. church decided to remain "out" and form a new congregation, at first meeting in the Lesser Town Hall. In 1930 the first minister, Revd. J.F. MacDonald, was ordained, and by 1939 a new church building was erected in Glaisnock Street, designed and built by Donald MacDonald. At the opening ceremony on 3rd June 1939 200 members turned up to hear a sermon by Revd. Robert Brakenridge, Moderator of the Presbytery. In 1959 the church was renamed St Andrew's U.F. Church.

STEVENSONS OFFICES — This building is currently owned by Stevensons Dairy Farms and is used as offices for the company. The building was originally erected between 1897 and 1904 by the Crichton family of Hillside House as three shop premises. The Crichtons had given money for the erection of Crichton Memorial Church adjacent, designed by the same architect, David Menzies of Edinburgh. The Victorian frontage is a particularly attractive feature.

HAMILTON PLACE — This attractive row of shops was built in 1903 and the shops opened in April 1904. Today only that originally occupied by Goldie's bears any resemblance to the picture, the others being bought by the Auchinleck Co-operative Society which in April 1956 converted it into a double-storey shop. Original occupants of the shops were, Goldie the tailor's, John Andrew, chemist, Misses A and M Bryce, drapers, Miss Grace Sampson, draper, Thomas MacGauchie, barber, and Hugh Black, solicitor.

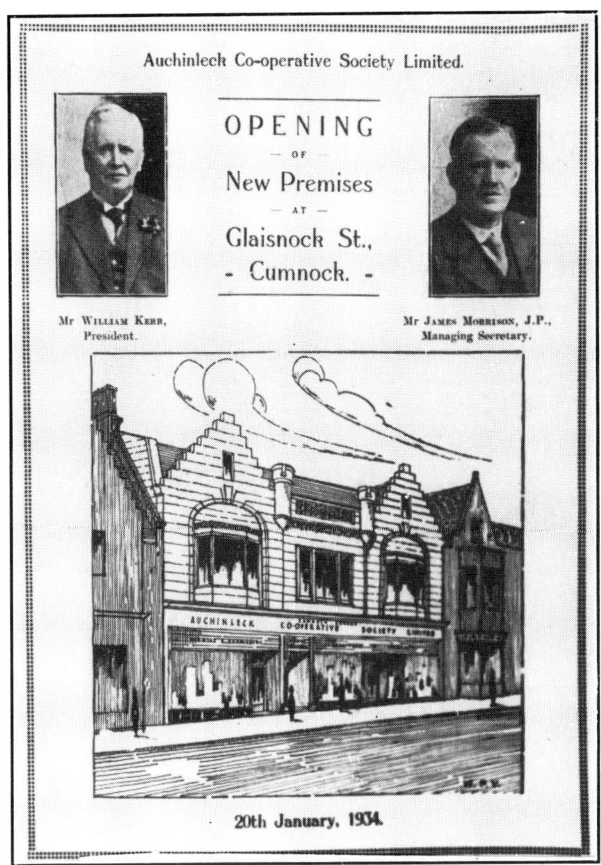

CO-OP BUILDING — The new branch of the Auchinleck Co-Operative Society erected in Glaisnock Street was officially opened on 20th January 1934 by William Kerr, President of the Society. Comprising a grocery, pharmacy and furnishing salon, the building was designed in neo-baronial style by W.F. Valentine, who had worked for the Auchinleck Co-Op previously. The building work was done by S. Connell, Dickson & Co, Shankland & Turnbull, and other firms. The evening before the opening ceremony a concert was held in the building, and a lunch followed in the Lesser Town Hall.

GREENHOLM LAUNDRY — Seen here are some of the workers inside the Greenholm Laundry, which was located near MacCartney's engineering works. The building was originally a weaving factory (from 1870) but was converted into a steam laundry.

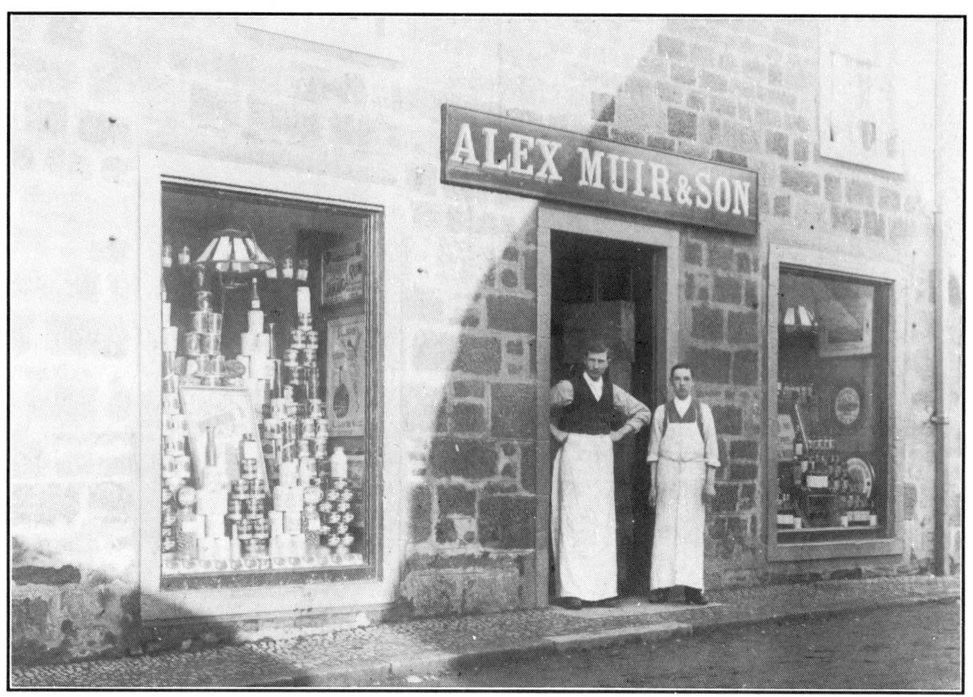

ALEX MUIR & SON — Alexander Muir established his family grocery and wine merchant's business in 1859 and set up shop at 9 Townhead Street. These two photographs depict the shop at different stages of development. Standing at the doorway above is William Laurie of Auchinleck, who worked for the firm for 62 years. The other person is unknown. Grandfather Alex came from Paisley to Cumnock and was regarded as "Cumnock's first practical grocer, in the modern acceptance of the term." He was a keen member of the 12th Ayrshire Rifles, and was one of the nine who signed the petition which led to the formation of Cumnock Burgh. He died in 1886, and was followed by his son, James, who died in 1914,

succeeded by Alex. From old advertisements we note that they sold "a first-class stock of groceries and provisions at city prices," and whisky, "either as a beverage, a stimulant or for Medicinal purposes." Muir's sold their own special blend of whisky, labelled "Corsegellioch" after the hill to the south of Cumnock. It was a blend of Ardbeg, Islay and Cambus malts, bottled on the premises and sold at sixpence per gill. The business was closed in April 1964, Alex Muir dying a week beforehand.

LIVINGSTONES — Both these pictures show James Livingstone's grocery and spirits shop at different stages of development. Note the change in how his name was spelled. The business was founded in 1861 by Mrs Janet Livingstone, followed by Robert then James. Mrs Livingstone's first shop was located further down Lugar Street, in the thatched cottage seen on the right of the photograph of Lugar Street on page 70. She moved into the premises shown above (number 15) around 1880. The upper photograph is older, showing David Connell and senior assistant David Hannah by the door. The adjoining shops, formerly owned by John Baird, were taken over by Livingstone's and the shop extended. The lower picture shows the assistants posing in front of the new facade just prior to the Great War. From left to right: Alex Lindsay, David Connell, Mrs Kay, Robert Livingstone, and David MacCulley. In 1967 the Livingstone's sold the shop, but it continued to trade under that name until 1982.

S & A GALBRAITH - GROCERS — The Galbraith's established their grocery business in Cumnock in 1849, firstly in the Square. In 1890 Samuel Galbraith bought some old buildings at the corner of Tower Street and Elbow Lane which he converted into a large grocery shop. To its rear he erected a new factory in which confectionery and jams were made. Samuel Galbraith acted as a councillor from 1901-1904. The two photographs depict two different means of delivery, the upper photograph of a van parked in front of the West Kirk, around 1910, the lower of a minivan and trailer. The Galbraith shop was demolished in the late 1960s, by which time it was owned by Spence Galbraith. Galbraith's established a cash and carry in a new building erected in Cairn Road in December 1970 as part of the Mace group.

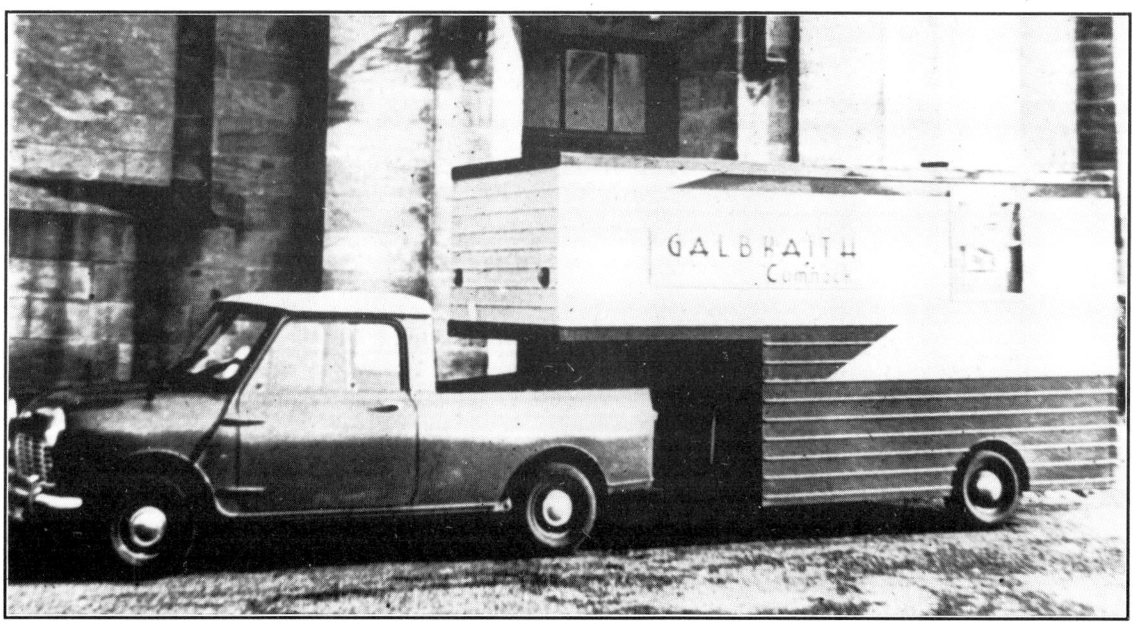

DRILL HALL — The 12th Ayrshire Rifle Volunteer Corps originally met in the small hall over the Dumfries Arms Stables. In 1908, when the County Association became responsible for the Territorial Army, plans were made for a new hall at Townhead, being almost complete at the outbreak of war in 1914. It had a large drill hall, armoury, miniature shooting range, recreation room and office accomodation. A new drill hall was erected in 1957. The hall is now used as business premises, and also by the Junior football team and Cumnock and District Camera Club.

RIFLEMAN'S BRIDGE — The Rifleman's Bridge was located in Glen Lugar, crossing the Lugar Water from the old Logan Quarry near Longhouse to the Holm Ironstone Pit, below Roadinghead. The bridge was erected by George MacCartney's Engineering Works. The span was 75 feet and it was used by the Territorial Army to reach the targets on Broom Braes. Shots could be fired from 200, 500 or 600 yards, the latter at Longhouse. The bridge was removed in 1920 and relocated at Greenholm, adjacent to Joe's Bridge, and used until the present bridge was erected in 1930. Joe's Bridge was removed on 11th October 1967.

WAR MEMORIAL — Located in the new cemetery, the Cumnock War Memorial was unveiled in 1921 to commemorate the 117 men who were killed in the Great War, 1914-1919. Built of white granite, it has bronze panels. From the parish 662 men had enlisted for service and sixteen of them were decorated for outstanding service. In 1950 an additional wall was added on which the names of a further 37 soldiers who gave their lives in the Second World War were inscribed. Many of the churches erected plaques to commemorate the dead from congregation, and the old Academy in Barrhill Road has a memorial.

POLICE STATION — This photograph shows the old police station in Townhead Street, erected in 1839 as the Court House of the Justices of the Peace who had met previously in the school in the Square, which had a jail attached. In 1858 the Ayrshire Constabulary was formed and part of the Townhead building was converted into a police station. A new court house was erected to the rear of the old building in 1895. The police station remained here until 29th November 1972 when business was transferred to the new station in Ayr Road, opened by James Jennings. Designed by Clark Fyfe, it cost £125,000.

MURRAY PARK — The Murray Park was opened on 21st September 1929 by Mrs Hyslop of Bank House. The funds for the park were left to the inhabitants of the parish by the Misses Agnes and Annie Murray who had owned the Dumfries Arms. The bequest was left to the people in 1917 and a Murray Trust established, operated by the Parish Council. The ten acre park was laid out on the lands of Netherthird, just outwith the burgh boundary, and had swings, various roundabouts, playing pitches, and walks by the side of the Glaisnock and Holm Burn. The trust are still responsible for the park.

DRUMBROCHAN GOLF COURSE — Golf has been played at various places in the parish over the years, including near Ayr Road and Cairn Road. In 1900 a nine-hole course was laid out at Netherthird but this land was later required for housing. In 1922 the course at Drumbrochan was opened, the greenkeeper's hut located at the old Drumbrochan farm. In 1954 this course was also needed for building, when Holland Crescent and Dalgleish Avenue were built. The council held a vote which decided 229 to 94 against establishing a municipal course, meaning that the parish has no facilities for golf.

GLAISNOCK STREET — The shops shown here were demolished to give access to the new shopping centre. William Carle had a drapery, previously occupied by Alexander White and James Breckenridge. Next door was a baker's, originally MacKechnie's, but latterly was MacCall's fruit shop. Next was Miss Miller's sweet shop, followed by Jenny MacGavin who sold ice cream. MacCormick's shoe-shop followed, latterly Gilmour's bakery. The shop with the sun-shade was George Scott's, Livingstone Hastings', William Auld's then Hugh Climie's butcher's. The last shop below the Dutch gables was Mrs Brown's baby linen shop.

PAST ALLAN'S CLOCK — Taken in 1961, the first shop past the Dutch gables (with sun-shade out) was Lipton's grocery, previously a drapery. Next door was Wilson's grocery, latterly becoming part of Lipton's. Left of the clock was Ballantine's printery and stationers, latterly MacKechnie's, who had a toy showroom upstairs. Turnbull and Allan were watchmakers next door. It was latterly Margaret Lindsay's drapery. The clock was a gift from a native in 1918. It was knocked off the wall July 1963 by a double-decker bus. A replacement was put up in 1965, but was relocated on the Co-operative building.

NEW BRIDGE STREET — This short stretch of roadway between Ayr Road and the Meetinghouse Bridge (at the Dubb) is known as New Bridge Street. The New Bridge was erected in the late 18th century, to replace the old Dubb Ford across the Glaisnock. This bridge remained until 1964 when the present bridge was erected, prior to the redevelopment of the Tanyard as a main thoroughfare. On the right is Cowan and Panton's garage, latterly Gaulds, and now a council garage. The little shop on the left was Jim Ewen's general merchant store.

THE A & C LINE — This picture shows a long train of empty coal waggons parked on the Ayr and Cumnock branch line prior to its closure. The small bridge allowed cattle to pass between fields belonging to Glengyron farm. Within the sweep of the railway is Glenramskill and Glencairn, the site of the old Shankston ironstone pit being located between them, now a small play area.

2ND CUMNOCK GIRL GUIDES — The cheery group shown are the 2nd Cumnock Girl Guides whilst at camp near Strathaven in 1950. The first company of Girl Guides was formed in the town in 1924 and in 1935 the Guides joined with the Scouts to meet in the new wooden hall behind Millbank House. The Scouts were first established in 1908 but did not last. A more successful troop was formed in 1921, but this too has become defunct, the hall now used by 1st Cumnock Company of the Boys' Brigade, founded in 1962. The first Boys' Brigade company in the town was actually started by the Old Church in 1895, but became dormant.

VIEW TO BARSHARE — Taken when the old railway was being lifted, this picture looks towards the new housing scheme at Barshare. Designed by Sir Robert Matthew of Matthew, Johnson-Marshall & Partners, it was erected from 1957 onwards in phases, the first phase completed in August 1962. That year it won the Saltire Society Award for the best designed Local Authority housing in Scotland, but the lack of streets and access to some houses has since proved troublesome. Part of the scheme incorporated old cobbles brought from Glasgow to build walls and pave some open areas.

CUMNOCK ACADEMY — The New Academy was created out of the old Greenmill Primary School, the two schools swapping locations in 1969, causing much confusion regarding names thereafter. Greenmill school was erected in 1952-54, extended in 1964 and 1970 (by which time it was the Acadmey) by Clark Fyfe, the county architect, and the Social and Recreation Wing was added in 1971. Capable of accomodating up to 1,800 pupils, only one or two scholars could win the annual Sir John Latta Dux Medal. Latta was born at Darmalloch in the parish and became a wealthy shipping magnate with Lowther, Latta and Company.

ST CONVAL'S HIGH SCHOOL — In 1886 Lord Bute donated money towards the erection of a new school for Roman Catholics in the parish, to replace an old building at Benston. Named St John's, the building was constructed of iron and wood and was located in Bank Avenue. In 1907 a more substantial building was erected, again with Bute aid, and the teaching was done by the Sister Servants of the Sacred Heart. St Conval's J.S. School was opened in 1961, seen here from Stepends Bing. The first headmaster was Thomas Finn, provost of Cumnock from 1966 to 1969, followed by Dante Filippi and Brendan Dorrian.

CAPONACRE — A few different locations for factories around Cumnock were considered before Caponacre was decided upon as the main industrial estate. At the sites considered factories were erected, such as Sykes Hatchery in Auchinleck Road, opened in October 1964, or the Bata Shoe factory at Skerrington Mains in 1964. At Caponacre a carpet factory was erected in 1967 and Galbraiths Cash and Carry in Cairn Road in 1970. A branch of Scottish Aviation was set up followed by Falmer Jeans, and a carpet yarn spinner. The Caponacre estate has been extended a few times since with smaller units.

BROOMFIELD PLAYING FIELDS — The thirty acres of Broomfield farm were bought in 1962 by the council and pitches laid out for football, rugby, cricket and running. In September 1967 the unusual pavilion was opened in the middle of the park for changing purposes, with an upstairs refreshment room with viewing windows on three sides. The park is used by the adjacent secondary schools throughout the year, and Cumnock Rugby Football Club has its home ground here. This club has the former Broomfield Farm as its clubhouse. In 1991 facilities for field events were created.

CUMNOCK JUNIORS FOOTBALL CLUB — The 'Nock were founded in 1913, the main founders being William MacMillan, Joe Bain and Tom Burns. They played at New Station Park, the first game in August against Cronberry resulting in a 3-3 draw. This park was located behind the new cemetery but in 1934, when ground was required for an extension to the burial ground, they moved to Townhead Park, which has been their home since. The bing was utilised in 1950 for terracing and in 1955 a grandstand built. In 1950 Cumnock reached the final of the Scottish Junior Cup, but were beaten by Blantyre. The team, shown above, was T. Hunter, J. McCartney, E. Nash, J. McCulloch, Bertie Knox, P. MacDonald, J. Stewart, M. MacLeod, John Cleland, A. Duncan, and P. Yuill.

On 19th May 1979 the Juniors again reached the Scottish final, playing against Bo'ness at Hampden. Cumnock's Flynn headed the ball into the net in the second half, the only goal of the match. The players returned to an ecstatic town. They were - Bentley, W. Paton, Barrowman, Reynolds, McCulloch, MacAnespie, Dickson, J. Docherty, Flynn, and Murray. The Juniors reached the final again in 1989, managing to beat Ormiston Primose 1-0 at Rugby Park, Derek Love scoring.

CHANGUE FARM — Changue farm was originally owned by the Boswells of Garrallan but was tenanted by the Stevenson family from 1867 until they bought it in 1920. With Crofthead, this created a farming unit of 275 acres, a further 460 acres at Newfield. In 1943 Bankend was leased from the Marquis of Bute. Since 1906 the Changue herd of Ayrshire cattle has been pedigreed and in 1936 a milk bottling plant was erected. In the same year the first Farmer's Milk bar was opened. John Stevenson ran the company from 1932 until his death in 1975. He had been awarded the MBE in 1951.

HARVESTING AT BANKEND — This pleasant scene shows harvesters at work on Bankend farm in the summer of 1963. The farm was leased to Stevenson of Changue at the time of the photograph, but in recent years has returned to Bute management, the steading demolished to make way for housing, the large farmhouse of 1855 saved. In the middle distance is a view of Cumnock in its hollow of the hills. Distinctive buildings include the Dumfries Arms, Crichton West spire, bus garage, and knitwear factory. The newly erected houses at Barshare can be made out, and also the gasometer which stood in Greenholm Road.

CUMNOCK CARNIVAL — The annual Carnival was instituted in 1946 by a local committee to celebrate the victory in the war. It was such a success that it was repeated each year thereafter. The parade started in Barrhill Road and the floats, up to two dozen or so, and bands toured through the streets to finish at the Woodroad where the Queen was crowned. The queen was originally chosen at a local dance, but from 1960 was chosen from schoolgirls. These photographs depict two of the main aspects of the carnival which remain in memories - the coronation and the floats. The Carnival Queen was Netta Smith, seen here in 1949 with her lady in waiting. The man standing is Robert Lachlan, the girl Sheila Gillies, next to Mrs Herbert Morton, wife of the Picture House proprietor. The bottom picture shows the Emrys Avenue float "Mary, Mary, Quite Contrary" of 1952. From right to left is Sheila Gillies, Cynthia Orr, Margaret Stevenson and Margaret MacTurk. Sheila Gillies just happens to be the author's mother! Children born on Carnival Day were presented with a commemorative cup. The carnivals became less popular but in recent years have been replaced by the Cumnock Juniors' Gala Days which try to recreate the excitement and splendour.

ROYAL VISIT - 1956 — A Royal Tour of Ayrshire was made in July 1956 by Her Majesty Queen Elizabeth and H.R.H. the Duke of Edinburgh. Cumnock was included on this sojourn, the Queen and Prince Philip arriving by train on the 3rd and met officially at a specially-built dais in Woodroad Park by Provost John Edgar. They toured a few places in the burgh and left by train later in the day. The Queen's son and heir, Prince Charles, has also visited the town. On 18th February 1943 King George VI came to Cumnock to watch the army doing river-crossing exercises at the Holm.

THE SURGERY — The present surgery in Townhead Street was opened in 1959, the first doctors to practise there being A.M. Campbell, James MacMillan and R.J.I. Boyd. Another surgery had existed at Millbank, where Doctors J.R. MacClure, H.C.J. MacLean and C.D. Rigg had their practise. Even earlier, their surgery was located in the upper floors of what had been the house of William MacLatchie, joiner, at 61 Glaisnock Street. Doctors MacLean and Rigg later moved to the new health centre at Auchinleck.

PUSHBALL — When the cyclists' rallies were held in the Woodroad Park, under the auspices of the Cumnock Ramblers' Cycling Club, this most unusual and unique sport was a favourite. Teams of around six or eight from different clubs would vie with each other to try and push the large steel ball to the opposite end of the field, and thus winning a point. Because of the size of the ball, and its habit of suddenly spinning round, the game was more difficult than it would appear. This photograph shows two teams battling it out at the rally of 1952.

AYRSHIRE BAKERIES — These buildings were originally a water mill, known as Sandbed Mill. It was powered by a lade from a weir across the Lugar known as the Minister's Dam. Alexander Duncan was the miller until 1692 followed by George MacGawn then his son John MacGawn. The mill buildings were later converted into a bakehouse which in 1963 went on fire. The photograph shows the firemen dowsing the flames. The buildings were latterly used by the council for storing their refuse lorries before they were demolished and Warrick Court sheltered housing built by the Bield Housing Association.

CLASS OF LESSER TOWN HALL — The old academy was forever failing to be large enough to accommodate all its pupils. This class was housed for a time in the lesser hall of the Town Hall, but the picture was taken in the early 1950s at the Barrhill. Back left to right: Robert Bradford, Andrew Stevenson, Sam Fitsimmons, Andrew Gilmour, Ronald Rutherford, George Veitch, Andrew Blackwood, Hector Milligan, Jim Blackwood, Ronnie Caldow. 2nd Back: Jim Dick, Jim MacCall, Allan MacCall, Robert Cockburn, William Paterson, John Sommerville, George MacLean, William Fleming, Jim Nisbet. Back row of girls: Sheila Carle, Isobel Weir, Maureen MacCall, Marion MacLean, Robert Wight, Ferris Vallance, Famie MacLeay, Elizabeth Adamson, Doris Arnott, Nan Meikle, Rona MacGee. 2nd Row: Sheila Donnan, Betty Dunlop, Margaret Veitch, Anne Weir, Agnes Orr, Margaret White, Anna Murray, Jean Nimmo, Nessie Gilmour, Dorothy Wallace. Front Row: Barbara Kelly, Rena Black, Margaret Moyle. Jean Taylor and Moira Thorburn were absent!

GLAISNOCK SCHOOL — From 1952 until 1973 Glaisnock House was run as a rural school, where boys received an eduction geared towards an agricultural vocation. This photograph of around 1963, shows: Back left to right: John Neil, Wallace Gyles, Robert Purdie, Ian Hamilton, Alex Maxwell, Duncan Borthwick, Jim Brown, Hugh Connel, William McGhee. 3rd Row: Jim Hunter, Jim Boswell, Jim Hunter, Tom Bradford, Hugh MacNish, John Nairn, William Murray, James Bond, William Hunter. 2nd Row: James Ramsay, Andrew Walker, George Caldwell, Campbell McPhie, Adam Sloan, Adam Wilson, Muir Craig, Ian Brown, John Guild, Angus Pettigrew. Front Row: William Raphael, Robert Wilson, Martin MacConnel, Robert Andrews, Andrew Aitken, John Blackwood, Albert Nichol, William Smith.

THE WESTERN BUS — Taken in the 1930s, this picture shows an old Western Omnibus sitting at the bottom of the Barrhill. The conductress was Mary Connor, later Mrs. Orr, the driver perhaps Jim Hyslop, Joe MacAlpine or Alex White. The shop on the left was the Hamilton Place branch of the Auchinleck Co-operative Society, prior to the erection of the upper floor. To the right of the bus can be made out the gable of James MacKibbin's shop where shoes were made and repairs done.

THE SALVATION ARMY — Taken next to the former wooden hut in Townhead Street which acted as the Salvation Army headquarters, this picture shows a number of the members. The Army arrived in Ayrshire in 1882 and in a short time had a number of members in Cumnock. The green hut was erected next to the police station in 1925, and remained in use until 1967. In that year the new hall was built further along Townhead Street, the large insignia on the wall being a distinctive feature. Membership at that time stood around 75. The site of the wooden hall is now occupied by the Bank of Scotland.

THE PREFABS — After the Second World War a shortage of houses and high number of uninhabitable dwellings spurred the council into building prefabricated houses. Forty of these were erected in Hearth Place, shown here. Although temporary buildings, they were actually kept longer than their lifespan dictated, and were eventually given a brick skin and pitched roof to create a most desirable bungalow. The photograph shows one of the last prefabs prior to conversion, with examples of the finished work around it.

1000TH COUNCIL HOUSE — The 1000th Council House built by the Burgh of Cumnock and Holmhead was erected in December 1954 at Drumbrochan. The actual house, to which a commemorative plaque was affixed, is at 2 Holland Crescent. This photograph shows the official opening, with Mr and Mrs Dick Gilmour, the first tenants, and council officials. By June 1970 the burgh had erected another five hundred houses and an inscribed stone was built into the wall of the flats of Meagher Court, also in Drumbrochan. The Right Honourable William Ross, Secretary of State for Scotland, declared that home open.

THE FLOOD OF 1966 — A number of floods have struck the town over the years, but that of 14th August 1966 was regarded as the "worst flood in Cumnock's history." Both the Glaisnock and Lugar waters burst their banks, flooding forty-two houses and causing chaos in the Glebe, Holm, and Greenholm. Fifteen hours of rain caused the rivers to rise an inch per minute, uprooting trees and destroying bridges. In some homes the water was three feet deep in the living room, leaving thick silt behind when the water subsided. Some folk who were evacuated were put up either in the Town Hall or Working Men's Club.

FLOOD AT GREENHOLM — This photograph shows an earlier flood than the large one in 1966. A number of floods have occurred over the years, in 1931, 1937, 1938, 1944, 1954, 1956, 1958, 1962 and 1963. Seen here are the two bridges which used to cross the river, the smaller Joe's Brig behind since removed. The row of single storey cottages in Townhead Street have been demolished, the site filled with the Richmond Terrace flats and split level houses, erected in 1961. In the top left of the photograph can be seen the Baptist Church, Urbana Terrace in the top right.

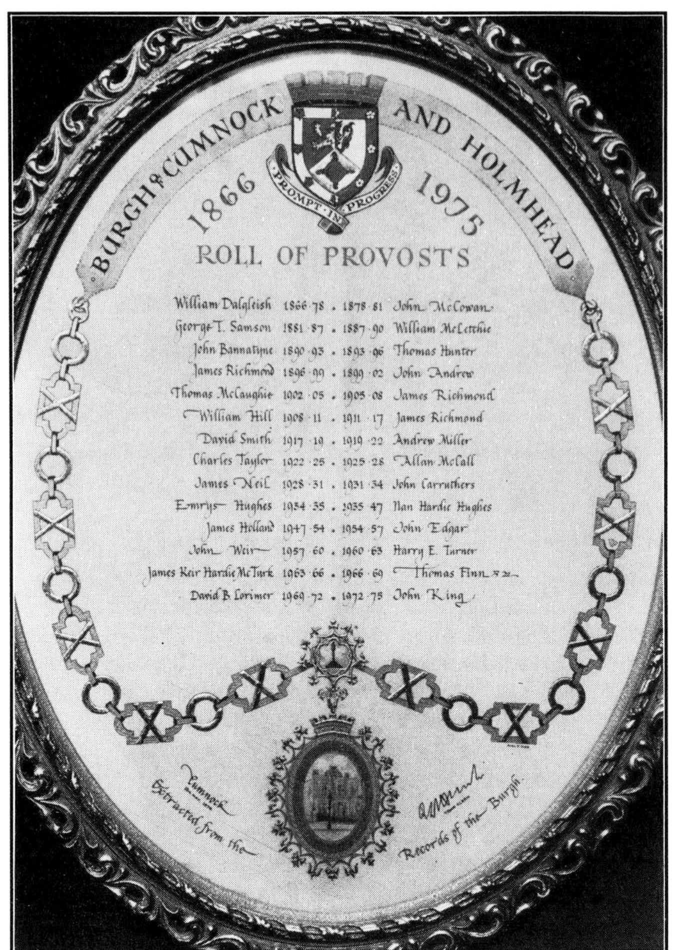

ROLL OF PROVOSTS — When the Burgh of Cumnock and Holmhead was established in 1866 the town had the right to elect police commissioners, one of whom became senior police magistrate. In 1892 this title was renamed provost, and in 1900 the commissioners became councillors. The first magistrate was William Dalgleish, woollen manufacturer, after whom Dalgleish Avenue was named. The last was John King, regionalisation in 1975 abolishing Small Burghs. The Roll of Provosts shown was made up in 1976 as a memento. James Richmond, a mason and builder, was the only person to hold the provostship more than once, he being provost three times. The lower photograph shows the Provost's Chain of Office, on which is a representation of the market cross and town hall. The chain was presented to the burgh in August 1916 by Alexander Gemmell to mark the burgh's golden jubilee. Gemmell was a local banker who settled in England and after whom Gemmell Avenue was named. In 1929 James Richmond, son of the old scavenger, engineer in Australia, donated money with which a gown, hat and chair was purchased for use of the provost. James Neil was formally robed with these on 12th August that year.

THE PAWN STEPS — Many corners of Cumnock have traditional names which unfortunately are being forgotten. The Pawn Steps is one of these, though more folk know this name than that of the Drummer's Brae, which was located at the foot of the steps. The steps lead from the Square down to Bank Lane and Tower Street, and were originally located in a narrow close between two buildings, one of which is demolished. Earlier, this gap was known as the Needle's E'e. With Caddie's Close, what became Lugar and Glaisnock streets and Hamilton Place, it was probably one of the old entrances to the kirkyard.

MINERS' STRIKE 1984 — The local mineworkers took part in the national strike from 9th March 1984 which lasted for almost a year, until 5th March 1985. The campaign was against suspected pit closures, an assumption which later turned out to be true, Killoch being closed in 1987 and the Barony in 1989. The workshops at Lugar were likewise closed, leaving the National Coal Board no operations in Ayrshire other than opencast workings. This photograph shows marchers with the Killoch banner in the Tanyard, heading for a rally at Broomfield at which the National Union of Mineworkers' president, Arthur Scargill, gave an address.

GLAISNOCK STREET — This view, taken from the Royal Hotel in 1973, shows Glaisnock Street just before the shops on the left were demolished to make way for the new shopping precinct. The architectural style of the buildings was quite unusual, particularly the use of Dutch gables. Last minute plans to prevent their demolition were unsuccessful. When the buildings were being razed an old well was discovered but unfortunately this was not built into the new concrete retaining walls, unlike the arch which supported one of the shops. This part of the town is called the Gorbals.

GLAISNOCK SHOPPING CENTRE — The top picture can be compared with this view of the Glaisnock Shopping Centre which was built on the site of Waterside Place and part of Townhead Street. Since opening a number of shops have come and gone, all part of the town's changing history. These include Galloway the butcher, Campbell the fruiterer, Castel San Angelo clothes shop, Drummond the chemist, the Job Centre, Lomond Wools, Spinning Stool crafts, Rowe's Delicatessen and Mrs Black's La Plaza cafe.

LARGEST ONION IN THE WORLD! — Bert Holland of Nan's Terrace in Cumnock is shown here with a Kelsae onion which he grew in his garden. Fed on organic fertiliser, the onion turned out to be the largest onion ever grown in the world, earning itself a place in the Guinness Book of Records. The onion weighed 11 pounds and 2 ounces, the previous record holder being 10 pounds and 14 ounces. It was at the National Kelsae Onion Festival at Harrogate in England that Bert, who had just grown onions for six years, discovered that his onion was a world-beater.

HILLSIDE SCHOOL — This view shows the new school erected at Drumbrochan for the education of children with profound or severe learning difficulties. A staff of seventeen (Margo MacFadzean as headmistress) teach children of between 2 and 17 years. The school was designed by Strathclyde architects and opened in March 1992, although the official opening did not take place until the following September. Built at a cost of one million pounds, the school incorporates a hydrotherapy pool. Hillside School replaced the former schools for the handicapped at Cronberry and Easton Place in Auchinleck.

HORSECLEUGH OPENCAST — Coal mining is a thing of the past in the parish of Old Cumnock, other than by opencast means. This photograph, taken in 1992, shows the proximity of the Horsecleugh opencast to the town, rising above the houses of Glaisnock Street. The small roadway rising up the hillside is the Cairn Brae, which was closed whilst working went on beneath it. This can be compared in size to the wider curving track which the huge dump trucks use to transport coal and overspill around the site. There had previously been opencasts at Bowes and Auchingilsie in the same locality.

THE CUMNOCK CHRONICLE — The Cumnock Chronicle is the longest lasting of a selection of former local newspapers. The Cumnock News was founded in 1880, the Cumnock Express in 1866. The Chronicle's first edition appeared on 8th November 1901, and the illustration right shows a fairly recent edition of 4th June 1992. The Chronicle has recorded Cumnock's history for almost a century, and the last six photographs in this book came from it, the work of staff photographer David Bingham, successor to John Merry.

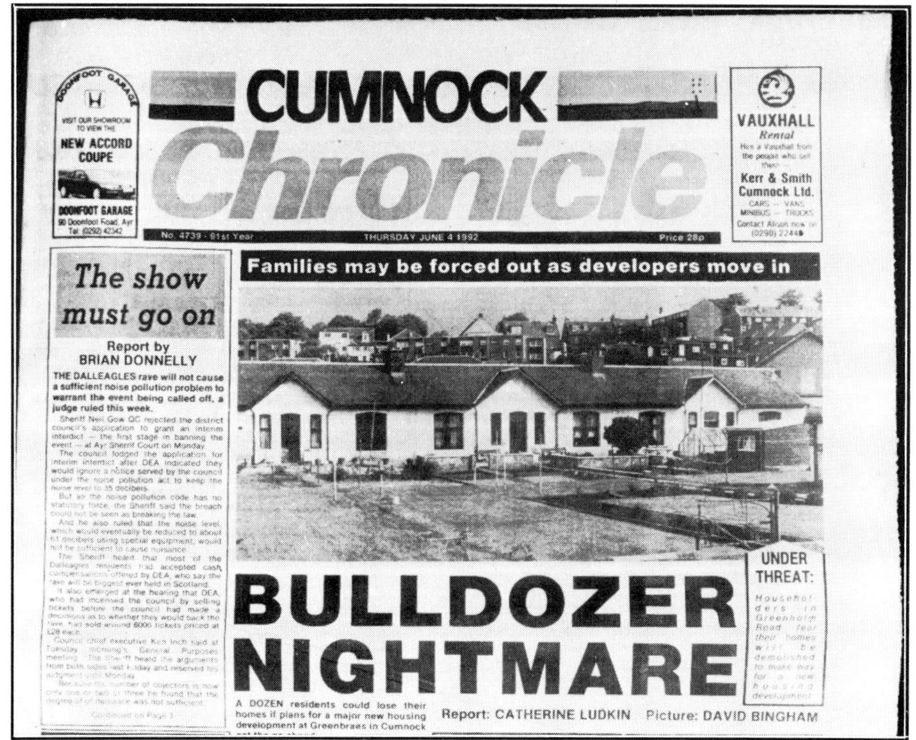

THE KEIR HARDIE CENTENARY — 1992 was the centenary of Keir Hardie's election to the House of Commons. A number of special events were organised for the year and these two photographs show some of the people involved. The upper picture illustrates Councillor Anna Boyd (left) standing with Jean Hardie Scott, Keir Hardie's granddaughter, and Dolores May Arias, his great granddaughter, at the bust in front of the Town Hall. Both relatives travelled from America to pay homage to their ancestor. The lower photograph shows a selection of Councillors and politicians outside the Baird Institute, which held a centenary exhibition, many artefacts belonging to the politician being left to the museum. From left to right they are: Alex Smith, Euro MP, Roy Hattersley MP, Anna Boyd, George Foulkes MP and David Sneller. A special church service was held in the Congregational Church (where Keir Hardie was a member) and plaques unveiled at Lochnorris, Baird Institute, Town Hall, New Cemetery and Bank Lane, where the newly landscaped grounds were named the Keir Hardie Memorial Gardens.